50 High-Protein Salad Recipes for Home

By: Kelly Johnson

Table of Contents

- Grilled Chicken Caesar Salad
- Steak and Blue Cheese Salad
- Shrimp and Quinoa Salad
- Tuna Nicoise Salad
- Greek Yogurt Chicken Salad
- Salmon and Avocado Salad
- Grilled Tofu and Edamame Salad
- Turkey Cobb Salad
- Lentil and Feta Cheese Salad
- Asian Sesame Chicken Salad
- Black Bean and Corn Salad with Grilled Chicken
- Egg and Spinach Salad with Turkey Bacon
- Chickpea and Roasted Vegetable Salad
- Seared Tuna and Mango Salad
- Greek Salad with Grilled Lamb
- Spinach and Mushroom Salad with Grilled Steak
- Quinoa and Roasted Vegetable Salad with Chicken
- Kale Caesar Salad with Grilled Shrimp
- Caprese Salad with Grilled Chicken
- Tofu and Broccoli Salad with Peanut Dressing
- Moroccan Spiced Chickpea Salad
- Seared Scallop and Mango Salad
- Turkey and Cranberry Quinoa Salad
- Grilled Halloumi and Watermelon Salad
- Southwest Black Bean and Chicken Salad
- Asian-Inspired Beef and Noodle Salad
- Edamame and Brown Rice Salad with Tofu
- Chicken and Mango Salad with Coconut Dressing
- Mediterranean Orzo Salad with Grilled Chicken
- Quinoa and Kale Salad with Lemon Herb Chicken
- Tofu and Avocado Salad with Miso Dressing
- Grilled Shrimp and Pineapple Salad
- Spinach and Strawberry Salad with Grilled Chicken
- Greek Pasta Salad with Turkey Sausage
- Roasted Vegetable and Chickpea Salad with Quinoa

- Thai Beef Salad with Peanut Dressing
- Chicken Caesar Pasta Salad
- Blackened Salmon and Mango Salad
- Lentil and Kale Salad with Grilled Chicken
- Quinoa and Black Bean Salad with Avocado
- Spinach and Goat Cheese Salad with Grilled Steak
- Chicken and Broccoli Salad with Sesame Dressing
- Roasted Cauliflower and Chickpea Salad with Tofu
- Greek Orzo Salad with Grilled Shrimp
- Asian-Inspired Tofu and Edamame Salad
- Turkey and Apple Salad with Honey Mustard Dressing
- Mediterranean Chickpea Salad with Feta
- Seared Tuna and Edamame Salad
- Southwest Quinoa Salad with Grilled Chicken
- Spinach and Bacon Salad with Hard-Boiled Eggs

Grilled Chicken Caesar Salad

Ingredients:

For the Grilled Chicken:

- 2 boneless, skinless chicken breasts
- 2 tablespoons olive oil
- Salt and pepper to taste
- 1 teaspoon garlic powder
- 1 teaspoon dried oregano
- 1 teaspoon paprika

For the Salad:

- 1 head romaine lettuce, chopped
- 1/2 cup Caesar salad dressing (store-bought or homemade)
- 1/4 cup grated Parmesan cheese
- 1 cup croutons (store-bought or homemade)

Instructions:

1. Preheat your grill to medium-high heat.
2. In a small bowl, mix together the olive oil, salt, pepper, garlic powder, oregano, and paprika to create a marinade for the chicken.
3. Place the chicken breasts in a resealable plastic bag or shallow dish, and pour the marinade over them. Make sure the chicken is evenly coated. Let it marinate for at least 30 minutes, or ideally, up to 2 hours in the refrigerator.
4. Once the chicken has finished marinating, remove it from the marinade and discard any excess marinade.
5. Place the chicken breasts on the preheated grill and cook for 6-8 minutes per side, or until they are cooked through and have nice grill marks. The internal temperature of the chicken should reach 165°F (75°C).
6. While the chicken is grilling, prepare the salad. In a large bowl, toss the chopped romaine lettuce with the Caesar salad dressing until evenly coated.
7. Once the chicken is done cooking, remove it from the grill and let it rest for a few minutes before slicing it into strips.

8. Arrange the dressed romaine lettuce on serving plates or a large platter. Top with the sliced grilled chicken.
9. Sprinkle the grated Parmesan cheese over the salad and garnish with the croutons.
10. Serve immediately and enjoy your delicious Grilled Chicken Caesar Salad!

Feel free to customize your salad by adding additional toppings such as cherry tomatoes, sliced cucumbers, or roasted red peppers.

Steak and Blue Cheese Salad

Ingredients:

For the Steak:

- 1 lb (450g) steak (such as ribeye, sirloin, or flank steak)
- Salt and pepper to taste
- 2 tablespoons olive oil
- 2 cloves garlic, minced
- 1 teaspoon dried thyme (optional)
- 1 teaspoon paprika (optional)

For the Salad:

- 6 cups mixed salad greens (such as baby spinach, arugula, and romaine lettuce)
- 1 cup cherry tomatoes, halved
- 1/2 red onion, thinly sliced
- 1/4 cup crumbled blue cheese
- Balsamic vinaigrette dressing (store-bought or homemade)

Instructions:

1. Season the steak generously with salt and pepper on both sides.
2. In a small bowl, mix together the olive oil, minced garlic, dried thyme, and paprika (if using) to create a marinade for the steak.
3. Place the seasoned steak in a resealable plastic bag or shallow dish, and pour the marinade over it. Make sure the steak is evenly coated. Let it marinate for at least 30 minutes at room temperature, or ideally, up to 2 hours in the refrigerator.
4. Preheat your grill or grill pan to medium-high heat.
5. Remove the steak from the marinade and discard any excess marinade.
6. Grill the steak for about 4-6 minutes per side, or until it reaches your desired level of doneness. The cooking time will depend on the thickness of your steak and your preferred level of doneness. For medium-rare, the internal temperature should reach 130-135°F (54-57°C).

7. Once the steak is done cooking, transfer it to a cutting board and let it rest for a few minutes before slicing it thinly against the grain.
8. While the steak is resting, prepare the salad. In a large bowl, toss together the mixed salad greens, cherry tomatoes, and sliced red onion.
9. Divide the salad mixture among serving plates or a large platter.
10. Arrange the sliced steak on top of the salad.
11. Sprinkle the crumbled blue cheese over the salad.
12. Drizzle the salad with balsamic vinaigrette dressing, to taste.
13. Serve immediately and enjoy your flavorful and satisfying Steak and Blue Cheese Salad!

Feel free to customize your salad by adding additional toppings such as sliced avocado, toasted nuts, or dried cranberries.

Shrimp and Quinoa Salad

Ingredients:

For the Shrimp:

- 1 lb (450g) large shrimp, peeled and deveined
- 2 tablespoons olive oil
- 2 cloves garlic, minced
- 1 teaspoon paprika
- Salt and pepper to taste

For the Quinoa Salad:

- 1 cup quinoa, rinsed
- 2 cups water or broth
- 1 cup cherry tomatoes, halved
- 1/2 cucumber, diced
- 1/4 cup red onion, finely chopped
- 1/4 cup chopped fresh parsley
- 1/4 cup crumbled feta cheese (optional)
- Juice of 1 lemon
- 2 tablespoons olive oil
- Salt and pepper to taste

Instructions:

1. Cook the quinoa according to package instructions. Once cooked, fluff it with a fork and let it cool to room temperature.
2. In a large bowl, combine the cooked quinoa, cherry tomatoes, cucumber, red onion, and chopped parsley.
3. In a small bowl, whisk together the lemon juice, olive oil, salt, and pepper to make the dressing.
4. Pour the dressing over the quinoa salad and toss until well combined. If using feta cheese, gently fold it into the salad.
5. Season the shrimp with salt, pepper, minced garlic, and paprika.

6. Heat 2 tablespoons of olive oil in a large skillet over medium-high heat. Add the seasoned shrimp to the skillet and cook for 2-3 minutes per side, or until they are pink and cooked through.
7. Once the shrimp are cooked, remove them from the skillet and let them cool slightly.
8. To serve, divide the quinoa salad among serving plates or bowls. Top each serving with the cooked shrimp.
9. Garnish with additional chopped parsley and a sprinkle of feta cheese, if desired.
10. Serve immediately and enjoy your flavorful Shrimp and Quinoa Salad!

This salad is versatile and can be customized with your favorite vegetables and herbs. Feel free to add avocado, bell peppers, or olives for extra flavor and nutrition.

Tuna Nicoise Salad

Ingredients:

For the Salad:

- 1 lb (450g) baby potatoes, halved
- 4 large eggs
- 1/2 lb (225g) green beans, trimmed
- 1/2 cup cherry tomatoes, halved
- 1/4 cup Niçoise olives
- 4 cups mixed salad greens (such as baby spinach, arugula, and romaine lettuce)
- 2 (5 oz / 140g) cans of tuna, drained
- 2 tablespoons capers, drained
- 1/4 cup chopped fresh parsley (optional)
- Lemon wedges, for serving

For the Dressing:

- 1/4 cup extra virgin olive oil
- 2 tablespoons red wine vinegar
- 1 tablespoon Dijon mustard
- 1 clove garlic, minced
- Salt and pepper to taste

Instructions:

1. Place the baby potatoes in a pot of salted water. Bring to a boil, then reduce the heat and simmer for 10-15 minutes, or until the potatoes are fork-tender. Drain and let them cool slightly.
2. Meanwhile, bring a separate pot of water to a boil. Carefully add the eggs to the boiling water and cook for 8-10 minutes for hard-boiled eggs. Once cooked, transfer the eggs to a bowl of ice water to cool completely. Peel and quarter the eggs.
3. In the same pot of boiling water used for the eggs, blanch the green beans for 2-3 minutes, or until they are crisp-tender. Drain and immediately transfer them to a

bowl of ice water to stop the cooking process. Once cooled, drain and pat dry with paper towels.
4. In a small bowl, whisk together the ingredients for the dressing: olive oil, red wine vinegar, Dijon mustard, minced garlic, salt, and pepper. Set aside.
5. Arrange the mixed salad greens on a large serving platter or individual plates.
6. Arrange the cooked baby potatoes, quartered hard-boiled eggs, blanched green beans, cherry tomatoes, Niçoise olives, and canned tuna on top of the salad greens.
7. Drizzle the dressing over the salad or serve it on the side.
8. Garnish the salad with capers and chopped fresh parsley, if desired.
9. Serve the Tuna Niçoise Salad with lemon wedges on the side for squeezing over the salad.
10. Enjoy this classic French salad as a flavorful and satisfying meal!

Feel free to customize your Tuna Niçoise Salad with additional toppings such as anchovies, roasted bell peppers, or radishes.

Greek Yogurt Chicken Salad

Ingredients:

For the Chicken:

- 2 boneless, skinless chicken breasts
- 1 tablespoon olive oil
- 1 teaspoon dried oregano
- Salt and pepper to taste

For the Salad:

- 1 cup Greek yogurt (plain or flavored)
- 1/4 cup chopped cucumber
- 1/4 cup chopped red onion
- 1/4 cup chopped bell pepper (any color)
- 1/4 cup chopped cherry tomatoes
- 2 tablespoons chopped fresh dill
- Juice of 1/2 lemon
- Salt and pepper to taste
- Lettuce leaves or bread, for serving (optional)

Instructions:

1. Preheat your grill or grill pan to medium-high heat.
2. Season the chicken breasts with olive oil, dried oregano, salt, and pepper.
3. Grill the chicken breasts for 6-8 minutes per side, or until they are cooked through and no longer pink in the center. The internal temperature of the chicken should reach 165°F (75°C). Once cooked, remove the chicken from the grill and let it rest for a few minutes before slicing it into strips.
4. In a large mixing bowl, combine the Greek yogurt, chopped cucumber, red onion, bell pepper, cherry tomatoes, chopped fresh dill, lemon juice, salt, and pepper. Stir until all ingredients are well combined.
5. Add the sliced grilled chicken to the bowl with the Greek yogurt mixture and toss until the chicken is coated evenly.

6. Serve the Greek Yogurt Chicken Salad on a bed of lettuce leaves or as a sandwich filling between slices of bread, if desired.
7. Enjoy this protein-packed and flavorful chicken salad as a light and healthy meal option!

Feel free to customize your Greek Yogurt Chicken Salad by adding other ingredients such as chopped olives, crumbled feta cheese, or diced avocado. You can also serve it on top of a green salad or as a filling for wraps or pitas.

Salmon and Avocado Salad

Ingredients:

For the Salmon:

- 2 salmon fillets
- 1 tablespoon olive oil
- Salt and pepper to taste
- Lemon wedges for serving

For the Salad:

- 4 cups mixed salad greens (such as baby spinach, arugula, and romaine lettuce)
- 1 ripe avocado, sliced
- 1/2 cucumber, sliced
- 1/4 red onion, thinly sliced
- 1/4 cup cherry tomatoes, halved
- 2 tablespoons chopped fresh dill (optional)
- 2 tablespoons chopped fresh parsley (optional)
- 2 tablespoons capers (optional)

For the Dressing:

- 2 tablespoons extra virgin olive oil
- 1 tablespoon lemon juice
- 1 teaspoon Dijon mustard
- 1 clove garlic, minced
- Salt and pepper to taste

Instructions:

1. Preheat your grill or grill pan to medium-high heat.
2. Brush the salmon fillets with olive oil and season with salt and pepper.

3. Grill the salmon fillets for 4-5 minutes per side, or until they are cooked through and flake easily with a fork. Remove from the grill and let them rest for a few minutes.
4. In a small bowl, whisk together the ingredients for the dressing: extra virgin olive oil, lemon juice, Dijon mustard, minced garlic, salt, and pepper. Set aside.
5. In a large mixing bowl, combine the mixed salad greens, sliced avocado, sliced cucumber, thinly sliced red onion, and halved cherry tomatoes.
6. Drizzle the dressing over the salad and toss gently to coat all ingredients evenly.
7. Divide the salad mixture among serving plates.
8. Top each salad with a grilled salmon fillet.
9. Garnish with chopped fresh dill, chopped fresh parsley, and capers, if desired.
10. Serve the Salmon and Avocado Salad with lemon wedges on the side for squeezing over the salmon.
11. Enjoy this flavorful and nutritious salad as a light and satisfying meal!

Feel free to customize your Salmon and Avocado Salad by adding other ingredients such as sliced bell peppers, shredded carrots, or toasted nuts. You can also substitute the grilled salmon with smoked salmon if preferred.

Grilled Tofu and Edamame Salad

Ingredients:

For the Grilled Tofu:

- 1 block (14 oz / 400g) firm tofu, pressed and drained
- 2 tablespoons soy sauce
- 1 tablespoon rice vinegar
- 1 tablespoon sesame oil
- 1 clove garlic, minced
- 1 teaspoon grated ginger
- Salt and pepper to taste

For the Salad:

- 4 cups mixed salad greens (such as baby spinach, arugula, and romaine lettuce)
- 1 cup shelled edamame, cooked according to package instructions
- 1/2 cucumber, sliced
- 1/4 red onion, thinly sliced
- 1/4 cup shredded carrots
- 2 tablespoons chopped fresh cilantro (optional)
- 2 tablespoons chopped roasted peanuts or sesame seeds (optional)

For the Dressing:

- 2 tablespoons soy sauce
- 1 tablespoon rice vinegar
- 1 tablespoon sesame oil
- 1 teaspoon honey or maple syrup
- 1 teaspoon grated ginger
- 1 clove garlic, minced
- Salt and pepper to taste

Instructions:

1. Preheat your grill or grill pan to medium-high heat.
2. Cut the pressed tofu into slices or cubes, depending on your preference.
3. In a small bowl, whisk together the soy sauce, rice vinegar, sesame oil, minced garlic, grated ginger, salt, and pepper to create a marinade for the tofu.
4. Place the tofu slices or cubes in a shallow dish and pour the marinade over them. Let the tofu marinate for at least 15-30 minutes.
5. While the tofu is marinating, prepare the salad ingredients. In a large mixing bowl, combine the mixed salad greens, cooked edamame, sliced cucumber, thinly sliced red onion, shredded carrots, and chopped fresh cilantro (if using).
6. In a separate small bowl, whisk together the ingredients for the dressing: soy sauce, rice vinegar, sesame oil, honey or maple syrup, minced garlic, grated ginger, salt, and pepper. Set aside.
7. Once the tofu has finished marinating, grill it on the preheated grill or grill pan for 3-4 minutes per side, or until it has grill marks and is heated through.
8. Remove the grilled tofu from the grill and let it cool slightly.
9. To assemble the salad, divide the salad mixture among serving plates or bowls.
10. Top each salad with grilled tofu slices or cubes.
11. Drizzle the dressing over the salad or serve it on the side.
12. Garnish the salad with chopped roasted peanuts or sesame seeds, if desired.
13. Serve immediately and enjoy this flavorful and nutritious Grilled Tofu and Edamame Salad!

Feel free to customize your salad by adding other vegetables such as bell peppers, radishes, or cherry tomatoes. You can also add a squeeze of lime juice for extra freshness.

Turkey Cobb Salad

Ingredients:

For the Salad:

- 4 cups mixed salad greens (such as baby spinach, arugula, and romaine lettuce)
- 1 cup cooked turkey breast, diced or shredded
- 4 strips cooked bacon, crumbled
- 2 hard-boiled eggs, sliced
- 1 ripe avocado, diced
- 1/2 cup cherry tomatoes, halved
- 1/4 cup crumbled blue cheese or feta cheese
- 1/4 cup thinly sliced red onion
- 1/4 cup sliced cucumber
- 2 tablespoons chopped fresh chives or green onions
- Salt and pepper to taste

For the Dressing:

- 1/4 cup extra virgin olive oil
- 2 tablespoons red wine vinegar
- 1 teaspoon Dijon mustard
- 1 clove garlic, minced
- Salt and pepper to taste

Instructions:

1. In a large mixing bowl, combine the mixed salad greens, diced turkey breast, crumbled bacon, sliced hard-boiled eggs, diced avocado, halved cherry tomatoes, crumbled blue cheese or feta cheese, thinly sliced red onion, and sliced cucumber.
2. In a small bowl, whisk together the ingredients for the dressing: extra virgin olive oil, red wine vinegar, Dijon mustard, minced garlic, salt, and pepper.
3. Drizzle the dressing over the salad and toss gently to coat all ingredients evenly.
4. Season the salad with salt and pepper to taste.
5. Divide the Turkey Cobb Salad among serving plates or bowls.
6. Garnish each serving with chopped fresh chives or green onions.

7. Serve immediately and enjoy this flavorful and satisfying salad as a light and nutritious meal!

Feel free to customize your Turkey Cobb Salad by adding other ingredients such as sliced bell peppers, shredded carrots, or toasted nuts. You can also substitute the turkey breast with grilled chicken or smoked turkey if preferred.

Lentil and Feta Cheese Salad

Ingredients:

For the Salad:

- 1 cup dry green or brown lentils, rinsed
- 2 cups water or vegetable broth
- 1/2 red onion, finely chopped
- 1/2 cup chopped fresh parsley
- 1/4 cup chopped fresh mint
- 1/2 cup crumbled feta cheese
- 1/4 cup chopped sun-dried tomatoes (optional)
- Salt and pepper to taste

For the Dressing:

- 1/4 cup extra virgin olive oil
- 2 tablespoons red wine vinegar
- 1 teaspoon Dijon mustard
- 1 clove garlic, minced
- Salt and pepper to taste

Instructions:

1. In a medium saucepan, combine the rinsed lentils and water or vegetable broth. Bring to a boil, then reduce the heat to low and simmer for 20-25 minutes, or until the lentils are tender but still hold their shape. Drain any excess liquid and let the lentils cool to room temperature.
2. In a large mixing bowl, combine the cooked lentils, finely chopped red onion, chopped fresh parsley, chopped fresh mint, crumbled feta cheese, and chopped sun-dried tomatoes (if using).
3. In a small bowl, whisk together the ingredients for the dressing: extra virgin olive oil, red wine vinegar, Dijon mustard, minced garlic, salt, and pepper.
4. Drizzle the dressing over the salad and toss gently to coat all ingredients evenly.
5. Season the salad with salt and pepper to taste.

6. Serve the Lentil and Feta Cheese Salad chilled or at room temperature.
7. Enjoy this flavorful and nutritious salad as a light and satisfying meal or as a side dish!

Feel free to customize your Lentil and Feta Cheese Salad by adding other ingredients such as diced cucumbers, bell peppers, or olives. You can also sprinkle toasted nuts or seeds on top for extra crunch and nutrition.

Asian Sesame Chicken Salad

Ingredients:

For the Salad:

- 2 boneless, skinless chicken breasts
- Salt and pepper to taste
- 1 tablespoon olive oil
- 8 cups mixed salad greens (such as baby spinach, shredded cabbage, and romaine lettuce)
- 1 cup shredded carrots
- 1/2 cucumber, thinly sliced
- 1/4 cup chopped green onions
- 1/4 cup chopped cilantro
- 1/4 cup chopped peanuts or almonds
- 1 tablespoon sesame seeds (black or white), for garnish
- Lime wedges, for serving

For the Sesame Ginger Dressing:

- 3 tablespoons soy sauce
- 2 tablespoons rice vinegar
- 1 tablespoon sesame oil
- 1 tablespoon honey or maple syrup
- 1 teaspoon grated ginger
- 1 clove garlic, minced
- Salt and pepper to taste

Instructions:

1. Season the chicken breasts with salt and pepper on both sides.
2. Heat olive oil in a skillet over medium-high heat. Add the chicken breasts and cook for 6-8 minutes per side, or until they are golden brown and cooked through. Remove from the skillet and let them rest for a few minutes before slicing them thinly.

3. In a large mixing bowl, combine the mixed salad greens, shredded carrots, thinly sliced cucumber, chopped green onions, and chopped cilantro.
4. In a small bowl, whisk together the ingredients for the Sesame Ginger Dressing: soy sauce, rice vinegar, sesame oil, honey or maple syrup, grated ginger, minced garlic, salt, and pepper.
5. Drizzle the dressing over the salad and toss gently to coat all ingredients evenly.
6. Divide the dressed salad among serving plates or bowls.
7. Arrange the sliced chicken breast on top of each salad.
8. Garnish the salad with chopped peanuts or almonds and sesame seeds.
9. Serve the Asian Sesame Chicken Salad with lime wedges on the side for squeezing over the salad.
10. Enjoy this flavorful and nutritious salad as a light and satisfying meal!

Feel free to customize your Asian Sesame Chicken Salad by adding other ingredients such as sliced bell peppers, edamame, or mandarin oranges. You can also substitute the chicken with grilled shrimp or tofu if preferred.

Black Bean and Corn Salad with Grilled Chicken

Ingredients:

For the Grilled Chicken:

- 2 boneless, skinless chicken breasts
- 1 tablespoon olive oil
- 1 teaspoon chili powder
- 1 teaspoon ground cumin
- Salt and pepper to taste

For the Black Bean and Corn Salad:

- 1 (15 oz) can black beans, drained and rinsed
- 1 cup frozen corn, thawed
- 1/2 red bell pepper, diced
- 1/2 green bell pepper, diced
- 1/4 cup diced red onion
- 1/4 cup chopped fresh cilantro
- Juice of 1 lime
- 2 tablespoons extra virgin olive oil
- 1 teaspoon ground cumin
- Salt and pepper to taste

Instructions:

1. Preheat your grill or grill pan to medium-high heat.
2. Season the chicken breasts with olive oil, chili powder, ground cumin, salt, and pepper. Make sure the chicken is evenly coated with the seasoning.
3. Grill the chicken breasts for 6-8 minutes per side, or until they are cooked through and no longer pink in the center. Remove from the grill and let them rest for a few minutes before slicing them thinly.
4. In a large mixing bowl, combine the black beans, corn, diced red bell pepper, diced green bell pepper, diced red onion, and chopped fresh cilantro.

5. In a small bowl, whisk together the lime juice, extra virgin olive oil, ground cumin, salt, and pepper to make the dressing.
6. Pour the dressing over the black bean and corn salad and toss gently to coat all ingredients evenly.
7. Divide the salad among serving plates or bowls.
8. Arrange the sliced grilled chicken breast on top of each salad.
9. Garnish the salad with additional chopped cilantro, if desired.
10. Serve the Black Bean and Corn Salad with Grilled Chicken immediately and enjoy this flavorful and nutritious meal!

Feel free to customize your Black Bean and Corn Salad with Grilled Chicken by adding other ingredients such as diced avocado, cherry tomatoes, or sliced jalapeños. You can also serve it with a side of tortilla chips or over a bed of mixed greens.

Egg and Spinach Salad with Turkey Bacon

Ingredients:

For the Salad:

- 4 cups baby spinach leaves, washed and dried
- 4 hard-boiled eggs, peeled and sliced
- 4 slices turkey bacon, cooked and crumbled
- 1/2 cup cherry tomatoes, halved
- 1/4 cup sliced red onion
- 1/4 cup sliced cucumber
- 1/4 cup sliced mushrooms (optional)
- 2 tablespoons chopped fresh parsley or chives (optional)
- Salt and pepper to taste

For the Dressing:

- 3 tablespoons extra virgin olive oil
- 2 tablespoons red wine vinegar
- 1 teaspoon Dijon mustard
- 1 clove garlic, minced
- Salt and pepper to taste

Instructions:

1. In a large mixing bowl, combine the baby spinach leaves, sliced hard-boiled eggs, crumbled turkey bacon, halved cherry tomatoes, sliced red onion, sliced cucumber, and sliced mushrooms (if using). Toss gently to mix.
2. In a small bowl, whisk together the ingredients for the dressing: extra virgin olive oil, red wine vinegar, Dijon mustard, minced garlic, salt, and pepper.
3. Drizzle the dressing over the salad and toss gently to coat all ingredients evenly.
4. Season the salad with salt and pepper to taste.
5. Divide the salad among serving plates or bowls.
6. Garnish with chopped fresh parsley or chives, if desired.

7. Serve the Egg and Spinach Salad with Turkey Bacon immediately and enjoy this flavorful and nutritious meal!

Feel free to customize your Egg and Spinach Salad with Turkey Bacon by adding other ingredients such as sliced avocado, shredded carrots, or toasted nuts. You can also substitute the turkey bacon with regular bacon or cooked chicken if preferred.

Chickpea and Roasted Vegetable Salad

Ingredients:

For the Salad:

- 1 can (15 oz) chickpeas, drained and rinsed
- 2 cups mixed vegetables (such as bell peppers, zucchini, eggplant, cherry tomatoes, red onion), chopped into bite-sized pieces
- 2 tablespoons olive oil
- Salt and pepper to taste
- 4 cups mixed salad greens (such as baby spinach, arugula, and romaine lettuce)
- 1/4 cup crumbled feta cheese (optional)
- 2 tablespoons chopped fresh parsley or basil (optional)

For the Dressing:

- 3 tablespoons extra virgin olive oil
- 2 tablespoons balsamic vinegar
- 1 teaspoon Dijon mustard
- 1 clove garlic, minced
- Salt and pepper to taste

Instructions:

1. Preheat your oven to 400°F (200°C).
2. In a large mixing bowl, toss the mixed vegetables with olive oil, salt, and pepper until evenly coated.
3. Spread the vegetables in a single layer on a baking sheet lined with parchment paper.
4. Roast the vegetables in the preheated oven for 20-25 minutes, or until they are tender and lightly browned, stirring halfway through.
5. While the vegetables are roasting, prepare the dressing. In a small bowl, whisk together the extra virgin olive oil, balsamic vinegar, Dijon mustard, minced garlic, salt, and pepper until well combined. Set aside.

6. In a large mixing bowl, combine the drained and rinsed chickpeas with the mixed salad greens.
7. Once the roasted vegetables are done, add them to the bowl with the chickpeas and salad greens.
8. Drizzle the dressing over the salad and toss gently to coat all ingredients evenly.
9. Divide the salad among serving plates or bowls.
10. Garnish with crumbled feta cheese and chopped fresh parsley or basil, if desired.
11. Serve the Chickpea and Roasted Vegetable Salad immediately and enjoy this flavorful and nutritious meal!

Feel free to customize your Chickpea and Roasted Vegetable Salad by using your favorite vegetables or adding other ingredients such as avocado, olives, or toasted nuts. You can also serve it with a side of crusty bread or grilled chicken for a complete meal.

Seared Tuna and Mango Salad

Ingredients:

For the Seared Tuna:

- 2 tuna steaks, about 6 oz (170g) each
- 2 tablespoons soy sauce
- 1 tablespoon sesame oil
- 1 teaspoon grated ginger
- 1 clove garlic, minced
- Salt and pepper to taste
- 1 tablespoon olive oil (for searing)

For the Salad:

- 4 cups mixed salad greens (such as baby spinach, arugula, and romaine lettuce)
- 1 ripe mango, peeled and sliced
- 1/4 cup sliced red onion
- 1/4 cup chopped cucumber
- 1/4 cup chopped bell pepper (any color)
- 2 tablespoons chopped fresh cilantro
- 2 tablespoons chopped roasted peanuts or cashews (optional)

For the Dressing:

- 2 tablespoons lime juice
- 1 tablespoon soy sauce
- 1 tablespoon honey or maple syrup
- 1 tablespoon rice vinegar
- 1 tablespoon sesame oil
- 1 teaspoon grated ginger
- 1 clove garlic, minced
- Salt and pepper to taste

Instructions:

1. In a shallow dish, whisk together soy sauce, sesame oil, grated ginger, minced garlic, salt, and pepper. Add the tuna steaks to the marinade, turning to coat evenly. Let marinate for 15-30 minutes in the refrigerator.
2. In the meantime, prepare the salad ingredients. In a large mixing bowl, combine the mixed salad greens, sliced mango, sliced red onion, chopped cucumber, chopped bell pepper, and chopped fresh cilantro. Toss gently to mix.
3. In a small bowl, whisk together the ingredients for the dressing: lime juice, soy sauce, honey or maple syrup, rice vinegar, sesame oil, grated ginger, minced garlic, salt, and pepper. Set aside.
4. Heat olive oil in a skillet or grill pan over medium-high heat. Remove the tuna steaks from the marinade and discard any excess marinade. Sear the tuna steaks for 1-2 minutes on each side, or until desired doneness. The tuna should be seared on the outside and still pink in the center.
5. Remove the seared tuna from the skillet and let it rest for a few minutes before slicing thinly.
6. To assemble the salad, divide the salad mixture among serving plates or bowls. Top each salad with sliced seared tuna.
7. Drizzle the dressing over the salad or serve it on the side.
8. Garnish the salad with chopped roasted peanuts or cashews, if desired.
9. Serve the Seared Tuna and Mango Salad immediately and enjoy this flavorful and refreshing dish!

Feel free to customize your Seared Tuna and Mango Salad by adding other ingredients such as avocado slices, sliced radishes, or toasted coconut flakes. You can also adjust the dressing to suit your taste preferences by adding more or less honey, lime juice, or soy sauce.

Greek Salad with Grilled Lamb

Ingredients:

For the Grilled Lamb:

- 1 lb (450g) lamb chops or lamb loin chops
- 2 tablespoons olive oil
- 2 cloves garlic, minced
- 1 teaspoon dried oregano
- Salt and pepper to taste

For the Salad:

- 4 cups mixed salad greens (such as romaine lettuce, arugula, and spinach)
- 1 cucumber, diced
- 1 bell pepper, diced
- 1 cup cherry tomatoes, halved
- 1/2 red onion, thinly sliced
- 1/2 cup Kalamata olives, pitted
- 1/2 cup crumbled feta cheese
- 2 tablespoons chopped fresh parsley
- 2 tablespoons chopped fresh dill

For the Dressing:

- 1/4 cup extra virgin olive oil
- 2 tablespoons red wine vinegar
- 1 teaspoon Dijon mustard
- 1 clove garlic, minced
- 1 teaspoon dried oregano
- Salt and pepper to taste

Instructions:

1. Preheat your grill or grill pan to medium-high heat.
2. In a small bowl, whisk together olive oil, minced garlic, dried oregano, salt, and pepper. Coat the lamb chops with this mixture.
3. Grill the lamb chops for about 3-4 minutes per side for medium-rare, or longer according to your preference. Once cooked, remove from the grill and let them rest for a few minutes before slicing.
4. In a large salad bowl, combine the mixed salad greens, diced cucumber, diced bell pepper, halved cherry tomatoes, thinly sliced red onion, Kalamata olives, crumbled feta cheese, chopped fresh parsley, and chopped fresh dill.
5. In a small bowl, whisk together the ingredients for the dressing: extra virgin olive oil, red wine vinegar, Dijon mustard, minced garlic, dried oregano, salt, and pepper.
6. Pour the dressing over the salad and toss gently to coat all ingredients evenly.
7. Divide the salad among serving plates or bowls.
8. Top each serving with slices of grilled lamb.
9. Garnish with additional chopped fresh parsley and dill, if desired.
10. Serve the Greek Salad with Grilled Lamb immediately and enjoy this flavorful and satisfying dish!

Feel free to customize your Greek Salad with Grilled Lamb by adding other ingredients such as sliced avocado, roasted red peppers, or artichoke hearts. You can also serve it with a side of tzatziki sauce or warm pita bread.

Spinach and Mushroom Salad with Grilled Steak

Ingredients:

For the Grilled Steak:

- 2 steaks of your choice (such as ribeye, sirloin, or flank steak)
- 2 tablespoons olive oil
- 2 cloves garlic, minced
- 1 teaspoon dried thyme
- Salt and pepper to taste

For the Salad:

- 8 cups baby spinach leaves, washed and dried
- 1 cup sliced mushrooms (such as button or cremini)
- 1/4 cup thinly sliced red onion
- 1/4 cup crumbled blue cheese or goat cheese
- 1/4 cup chopped walnuts or pecans, toasted
- 1/4 cup dried cranberries or cherries (optional)

For the Balsamic Vinaigrette:

- 1/4 cup extra virgin olive oil
- 2 tablespoons balsamic vinegar
- 1 teaspoon Dijon mustard
- 1 clove garlic, minced
- Salt and pepper to taste

Instructions:

1. Preheat your grill or grill pan to medium-high heat.
2. In a small bowl, whisk together olive oil, minced garlic, dried thyme, salt, and pepper. Rub the steak with this mixture on both sides.

3. Grill the steak for about 4-5 minutes per side for medium-rare, or longer according to your preference. Once cooked, remove from the grill and let it rest for a few minutes before slicing.
4. In a large salad bowl, combine the baby spinach leaves, sliced mushrooms, thinly sliced red onion, crumbled blue cheese or goat cheese, chopped toasted walnuts or pecans, and dried cranberries or cherries (if using).
5. In a small bowl, whisk together the ingredients for the balsamic vinaigrette: extra virgin olive oil, balsamic vinegar, Dijon mustard, minced garlic, salt, and pepper.
6. Pour the balsamic vinaigrette over the salad and toss gently to coat all ingredients evenly.
7. Divide the salad among serving plates or bowls.
8. Slice the grilled steak and arrange it on top of each salad serving.
9. Serve the Spinach and Mushroom Salad with Grilled Steak immediately and enjoy this flavorful and satisfying meal!

Feel free to customize your Spinach and Mushroom Salad with Grilled Steak by adding other ingredients such as sliced avocado, roasted bell peppers, or croutons. You can also adjust the dressing to suit your taste preferences by adding more or less balsamic vinegar, Dijon mustard, or garlic.

Quinoa and Roasted Vegetable Salad with Chicken

Ingredients:

For the Roasted Vegetables:

- 2 cups mixed vegetables (such as bell peppers, zucchini, eggplant, cherry tomatoes, red onion), chopped into bite-sized pieces
- 2 tablespoons olive oil
- Salt and pepper to taste
- 1 teaspoon dried thyme (optional)
- 1 teaspoon dried rosemary (optional)

For the Chicken:

- 2 boneless, skinless chicken breasts
- 2 tablespoons olive oil
- 1 teaspoon paprika
- 1 teaspoon garlic powder
- Salt and pepper to taste

For the Quinoa:

- 1 cup quinoa, rinsed
- 2 cups water or chicken broth
- Salt to taste

For the Salad:

- 4 cups baby spinach leaves, washed and dried
- 1/4 cup crumbled feta cheese or goat cheese
- 1/4 cup chopped fresh parsley or basil
- 1/4 cup chopped walnuts or almonds, toasted (optional)
- 1/4 cup dried cranberries or cherries (optional)

For the Dressing:

- 1/4 cup extra virgin olive oil
- 2 tablespoons balsamic vinegar
- 1 teaspoon Dijon mustard
- 1 clove garlic, minced
- Salt and pepper to taste

Instructions:

1. Preheat your oven to 400°F (200°C).
2. In a large mixing bowl, toss the mixed vegetables with olive oil, salt, pepper, dried thyme, and dried rosemary until evenly coated.
3. Spread the vegetables in a single layer on a baking sheet lined with parchment paper.
4. Roast the vegetables in the preheated oven for 20-25 minutes, or until they are tender and lightly browned, stirring halfway through.
5. While the vegetables are roasting, prepare the chicken. In a small bowl, whisk together olive oil, paprika, garlic powder, salt, and pepper. Coat the chicken breasts with this mixture.
6. Heat a grill pan or skillet over medium-high heat. Cook the chicken breasts for about 6-8 minutes per side, or until they are cooked through and no longer pink in the center. Once cooked, remove from the heat and let them rest for a few minutes before slicing.
7. In a medium saucepan, combine the quinoa, water or chicken broth, and salt. Bring to a boil, then reduce the heat to low, cover, and simmer for 15-20 minutes, or until the quinoa is cooked and the liquid is absorbed. Remove from heat and let it sit, covered, for 5 minutes. Fluff with a fork.
8. In a large salad bowl, combine the baby spinach leaves, cooked quinoa, roasted vegetables, sliced chicken breasts, crumbled feta cheese or goat cheese, chopped fresh parsley or basil, toasted walnuts or almonds (if using), and dried cranberries or cherries (if using).
9. In a small bowl, whisk together the ingredients for the dressing: extra virgin olive oil, balsamic vinegar, Dijon mustard, minced garlic, salt, and pepper.
10. Drizzle the dressing over the salad and toss gently to coat all ingredients evenly.
11. Divide the salad among serving plates or bowls.

12. Serve the Quinoa and Roasted Vegetable Salad with Chicken immediately and enjoy this flavorful and nutritious meal!

Feel free to customize your Quinoa and Roasted Vegetable Salad with Chicken by using your favorite vegetables or adding other ingredients such as sliced avocado, roasted bell peppers, or crumbled bacon. You can also adjust the dressing to suit your taste preferences by adding more or less balsamic vinegar, Dijon mustard, or garlic.

Kale Caesar Salad with Grilled Shrimp

Ingredients:

For the Grilled Shrimp:

- 1 lb (450g) large shrimp, peeled and deveined
- 2 tablespoons olive oil
- 2 cloves garlic, minced
- 1 teaspoon paprika
- Salt and pepper to taste

For the Caesar Dressing:

- 1/2 cup mayonnaise
- 2 tablespoons grated Parmesan cheese
- 1 tablespoon lemon juice
- 1 teaspoon Dijon mustard
- 1 clove garlic, minced
- 1 anchovy fillet, finely chopped (optional)
- Salt and pepper to taste

For the Salad:

- 1 bunch kale, stems removed and leaves torn into bite-sized pieces
- 1 cup cherry tomatoes, halved
- 1/4 cup grated Parmesan cheese
- 1/4 cup croutons (optional)
- Lemon wedges, for serving

Instructions:

1. Preheat your grill or grill pan to medium-high heat.

2. In a large mixing bowl, toss the shrimp with olive oil, minced garlic, paprika, salt, and pepper until evenly coated.
3. Thread the shrimp onto skewers, if using, to make grilling easier.
4. Grill the shrimp for about 2-3 minutes per side, or until they are pink and opaque. Once cooked, remove from the grill and set aside.
5. In a small bowl, whisk together the ingredients for the Caesar dressing: mayonnaise, grated Parmesan cheese, lemon juice, Dijon mustard, minced garlic, anchovy fillet (if using), salt, and pepper. Adjust seasoning to taste.
6. In a large salad bowl, combine the torn kale leaves, halved cherry tomatoes, grated Parmesan cheese, and croutons (if using).
7. Pour the Caesar dressing over the salad and toss gently to coat all ingredients evenly.
8. Divide the salad among serving plates or bowls.
9. Top each serving with grilled shrimp.
10. Serve the Kale Caesar Salad with Grilled Shrimp immediately, with lemon wedges on the side for squeezing over the shrimp.
11. Enjoy this flavorful and nutritious salad as a light and satisfying meal!

Feel free to customize your Kale Caesar Salad with Grilled Shrimp by adding other ingredients such as sliced avocado, hard-boiled eggs, or crispy bacon. You can also use your favorite Caesar dressing recipe or store-bought dressing if preferred.

Caprese Salad with Grilled Chicken

Ingredients:

For the Grilled Chicken:

- 2 boneless, skinless chicken breasts
- 2 tablespoons olive oil
- 2 cloves garlic, minced
- 1 teaspoon dried basil
- Salt and pepper to taste

For the Salad:

- 2 large tomatoes, sliced
- 1 ball fresh mozzarella cheese, sliced
- Fresh basil leaves
- Balsamic glaze, for drizzling
- Salt and pepper to taste

Instructions:

1. Preheat your grill or grill pan to medium-high heat.
2. In a small bowl, mix together olive oil, minced garlic, dried basil, salt, and pepper.
3. Coat the chicken breasts with the mixture on both sides.
4. Grill the chicken breasts for about 6-8 minutes per side, or until they are cooked through and no longer pink in the center. Once cooked, remove from the grill and let them rest for a few minutes before slicing.

For the Salad:

1. On a large serving platter, alternate slices of tomato, fresh mozzarella, and fresh basil leaves, overlapping slightly.
2. Arrange the grilled chicken slices on top of the tomato and mozzarella.

3. Drizzle the salad with balsamic glaze.
4. Season with salt and pepper to taste.
5. Serve immediately and enjoy this refreshing and flavorful Caprese Salad with Grilled Chicken!

Feel free to customize your Caprese Salad with Grilled Chicken by adding extra ingredients such as avocado slices, roasted bell peppers, or olives. You can also use cherry tomatoes instead of large tomatoes for a different presentation.

Tofu and Broccoli Salad with Peanut Dressing

Ingredients:

For the Tofu and Broccoli:

- 1 block (14 oz) extra-firm tofu, pressed and cubed
- 2 cups broccoli florets
- 1 tablespoon olive oil
- Salt and pepper to taste

For the Salad:

- 6 cups mixed salad greens (such as baby spinach, arugula, and romaine lettuce)
- 1/4 cup shredded carrots
- 1/4 cup sliced red bell pepper
- 1/4 cup sliced cucumber
- 1/4 cup chopped green onions
- 2 tablespoons chopped fresh cilantro or parsley
- 2 tablespoons chopped roasted peanuts (optional)
- Lime wedges, for serving

For the Peanut Dressing:

- 1/4 cup creamy peanut butter
- 2 tablespoons soy sauce
- 1 tablespoon rice vinegar
- 1 tablespoon honey or maple syrup
- 1 clove garlic, minced
- 1 teaspoon grated ginger
- 1-2 tablespoons water, as needed to thin the dressing
- Salt and pepper to taste

Instructions:

1. Preheat your oven to 400°F (200°C).
2. In a large mixing bowl, toss the cubed tofu and broccoli florets with olive oil, salt, and pepper until evenly coated.
3. Spread the tofu and broccoli in a single layer on a baking sheet lined with parchment paper.
4. Roast in the preheated oven for 20-25 minutes, or until the tofu is golden brown and the broccoli is tender, stirring halfway through.
5. While the tofu and broccoli are roasting, prepare the salad ingredients. In a large salad bowl, combine the mixed salad greens, shredded carrots, sliced red bell pepper, sliced cucumber, chopped green onions, and chopped fresh cilantro or parsley.
6. In a small bowl, whisk together the ingredients for the peanut dressing: creamy peanut butter, soy sauce, rice vinegar, honey or maple syrup, minced garlic, grated ginger, salt, and pepper. Add water as needed to thin the dressing to your desired consistency.
7. Once the tofu and broccoli are done roasting, let them cool slightly.
8. Add the roasted tofu and broccoli to the salad bowl with the mixed greens and vegetables.
9. Drizzle the peanut dressing over the salad and toss gently to coat all ingredients evenly.
10. Divide the salad among serving plates or bowls.
11. Garnish with chopped roasted peanuts, if desired.
12. Serve the Tofu and Broccoli Salad with Peanut Dressing immediately, with lime wedges on the side for squeezing over the salad.
13. Enjoy this flavorful and nutritious salad as a light and satisfying meal!

Feel free to customize your Tofu and Broccoli Salad with Peanut Dressing by adding other ingredients such as sliced avocado, edamame, or toasted sesame seeds. You can also adjust the dressing to suit your taste preferences by adding more or less soy sauce, honey, or ginger.

Moroccan Spiced Chickpea Salad

Ingredients:

For the Salad:

- 2 cans (15 oz each) chickpeas, drained and rinsed
- 2 tablespoons olive oil
- 1 teaspoon ground cumin
- 1 teaspoon ground coriander
- 1/2 teaspoon ground cinnamon
- 1/4 teaspoon ground turmeric
- Salt and pepper to taste
- 1 cup diced cucumber
- 1 cup diced tomatoes
- 1/2 cup diced red onion
- 1/4 cup chopped fresh parsley
- 1/4 cup chopped fresh cilantro
- 1/4 cup chopped fresh mint
- 1/4 cup chopped roasted almonds or pistachios (optional)

For the Dressing:

- 1/4 cup extra virgin olive oil
- 2 tablespoons lemon juice
- 1 tablespoon honey or maple syrup
- 1 teaspoon ground cumin
- 1/2 teaspoon ground coriander
- 1/4 teaspoon ground cinnamon
- Salt and pepper to taste

Instructions:

1. Preheat your oven to 400°F (200°C).

2. In a large mixing bowl, toss the chickpeas with olive oil, ground cumin, ground coriander, ground cinnamon, ground turmeric, salt, and pepper until evenly coated.
3. Spread the seasoned chickpeas in a single layer on a baking sheet lined with parchment paper.
4. Roast in the preheated oven for 20-25 minutes, or until the chickpeas are crispy and golden brown, shaking the pan halfway through.
5. While the chickpeas are roasting, prepare the salad ingredients. In a large salad bowl, combine the diced cucumber, diced tomatoes, diced red onion, chopped fresh parsley, chopped fresh cilantro, and chopped fresh mint.
6. In a small bowl, whisk together the ingredients for the dressing: extra virgin olive oil, lemon juice, honey or maple syrup, ground cumin, ground coriander, ground cinnamon, salt, and pepper.
7. Once the chickpeas are done roasting, let them cool slightly.
8. Add the roasted chickpeas to the salad bowl with the mixed vegetables and herbs.
9. Drizzle the dressing over the salad and toss gently to coat all ingredients evenly.
10. Divide the salad among serving plates or bowls.
11. Garnish with chopped roasted almonds or pistachios, if desired.
12. Serve the Moroccan Spiced Chickpea Salad immediately and enjoy this flavorful and nutritious dish!

Feel free to customize your Moroccan Spiced Chickpea Salad by adding other ingredients such as diced bell peppers, olives, or raisins. You can also serve it with a side of couscous or quinoa for a complete meal.

Seared Scallop and Mango Salad

Ingredients:

For the Seared Scallops:

- 1 lb (450g) fresh scallops
- 2 tablespoons olive oil
- Salt and pepper to taste

For the Salad:

- 6 cups mixed salad greens (such as baby spinach, arugula, and romaine lettuce)
- 1 ripe mango, peeled and sliced
- 1/4 cup red onion, thinly sliced
- 1/4 cup chopped fresh cilantro
- 1/4 cup chopped roasted cashews or almonds
- 1/4 cup crumbled feta cheese (optional)
- Lime wedges, for serving

For the Dressing:

- 1/4 cup extra virgin olive oil
- 2 tablespoons lime juice
- 1 tablespoon honey or maple syrup
- 1 teaspoon Dijon mustard
- 1 clove garlic, minced
- Salt and pepper to taste

Instructions:

1. Pat the scallops dry with paper towels and season them with salt and pepper.
2. Heat olive oil in a skillet or non-stick pan over medium-high heat.

3. Add the scallops to the skillet and sear for about 2-3 minutes on each side, or until they are golden brown and cooked through. Be careful not to overcrowd the pan. Cook the scallops in batches if necessary.
4. Once cooked, remove the scallops from the skillet and set aside.
5. In a large salad bowl, combine the mixed salad greens, sliced mango, thinly sliced red onion, chopped fresh cilantro, chopped roasted cashews or almonds, and crumbled feta cheese (if using).
6. In a small bowl, whisk together the ingredients for the dressing: extra virgin olive oil, lime juice, honey or maple syrup, Dijon mustard, minced garlic, salt, and pepper.
7. Pour the dressing over the salad and toss gently to coat all ingredients evenly.
8. Divide the salad among serving plates or bowls.
9. Top each serving with seared scallops.
10. Serve the Seared Scallop and Mango Salad immediately, with lime wedges on the side for squeezing over the salad.
11. Enjoy this flavorful and refreshing salad as a light and satisfying meal!

Feel free to customize your Seared Scallop and Mango Salad by adding other ingredients such as avocado slices, cherry tomatoes, or sliced cucumber. You can also adjust the dressing to suit your taste preferences by adding more or less lime juice, honey, or Dijon mustard.

Turkey and Cranberry Quinoa Salad

Ingredients:

For the Salad:

- 1 cup quinoa, rinsed
- 2 cups water or vegetable broth
- 2 cups cooked turkey breast, diced
- 1/2 cup dried cranberries
- 1/4 cup chopped pecans or walnuts
- 1/4 cup chopped green onions
- 1/4 cup crumbled feta cheese or goat cheese (optional)
- 4 cups mixed salad greens (such as baby spinach, arugula, and romaine lettuce)

For the Dressing:

- 1/4 cup extra virgin olive oil
- 2 tablespoons apple cider vinegar
- 1 tablespoon maple syrup or honey
- 1 teaspoon Dijon mustard
- Salt and pepper to taste

Instructions:

1. In a medium saucepan, combine the quinoa and water or vegetable broth. Bring to a boil, then reduce the heat to low, cover, and simmer for 15-20 minutes, or until the quinoa is cooked and the liquid is absorbed. Remove from heat and let it sit, covered, for 5 minutes. Fluff with a fork and let it cool.
2. In a large mixing bowl, combine the cooked quinoa, diced turkey breast, dried cranberries, chopped pecans or walnuts, chopped green onions, and crumbled feta cheese or goat cheese (if using).
3. In a small bowl, whisk together the ingredients for the dressing: extra virgin olive oil, apple cider vinegar, maple syrup or honey, Dijon mustard, salt, and pepper.
4. Pour the dressing over the quinoa salad and toss gently to coat all ingredients evenly.

5. Arrange the mixed salad greens on a serving platter or individual plates.
6. Spoon the turkey and cranberry quinoa salad over the mixed greens.
7. Serve immediately and enjoy this delicious and nutritious Turkey and Cranberry Quinoa Salad!

Feel free to customize your Turkey and Cranberry Quinoa Salad by adding other ingredients such as sliced apples, celery, or toasted almonds. You can also adjust the dressing to suit your taste preferences by adding more or less maple syrup, apple cider vinegar, or Dijon mustard.

Grilled Halloumi and Watermelon Salad

Ingredients:

For the Salad:

- 8 oz (225g) halloumi cheese, sliced
- 4 cups cubed watermelon
- 2 cups mixed salad greens (such as arugula, spinach, and mint leaves)
- 1/4 cup sliced red onion
- 1/4 cup chopped fresh mint leaves
- 1/4 cup chopped pistachios or almonds
- Optional: additional herbs for garnish (such as basil or cilantro)

For the Dressing:

- 1/4 cup extra virgin olive oil
- 2 tablespoons balsamic vinegar
- 1 tablespoon honey or maple syrup
- 1 teaspoon Dijon mustard
- Salt and pepper to taste

Instructions:

1. Preheat your grill or grill pan to medium-high heat.
2. Grill the halloumi slices for about 1-2 minutes on each side, or until grill marks appear and the cheese is softened.
3. In a large mixing bowl, combine the cubed watermelon, mixed salad greens, sliced red onion, chopped fresh mint leaves, and chopped pistachios or almonds.
4. In a small bowl, whisk together the ingredients for the dressing: extra virgin olive oil, balsamic vinegar, honey or maple syrup, Dijon mustard, salt, and pepper.
5. Pour the dressing over the salad and toss gently to coat all ingredients evenly.
6. Arrange the grilled halloumi slices on top of the salad.
7. Optional: garnish with additional herbs such as basil or cilantro.
8. Serve the Grilled Halloumi and Watermelon Salad immediately and enjoy this flavorful and refreshing dish!

Feel free to customize your Grilled Halloumi and Watermelon Salad by adding other ingredients such as cucumber slices, cherry tomatoes, or avocado. You can also adjust the dressing to suit your taste preferences by adding more or less honey, balsamic vinegar, or Dijon mustard.

Southwest Black Bean and Chicken Salad

Ingredients:

For the Salad:

- 2 cups cooked chicken breast, shredded or diced
- 1 can (15 oz) black beans, drained and rinsed
- 1 cup corn kernels (fresh, frozen, or canned)
- 1 cup cherry tomatoes, halved
- 1 bell pepper (any color), diced
- 1/2 red onion, finely chopped
- 1 avocado, diced
- 1/4 cup chopped fresh cilantro
- 4 cups mixed salad greens (such as romaine lettuce, spinach, and arugula)
- Optional toppings: sliced jalapeños, diced avocado, shredded cheese, tortilla strips

For the Dressing:

- 1/4 cup extra virgin olive oil
- 2 tablespoons lime juice
- 1 tablespoon honey or maple syrup
- 1 teaspoon ground cumin
- 1/2 teaspoon chili powder
- 1/4 teaspoon garlic powder
- Salt and pepper to taste

Instructions:

1. In a large salad bowl, combine the cooked chicken breast, black beans, corn kernels, cherry tomatoes, diced bell pepper, finely chopped red onion, diced avocado, and chopped fresh cilantro.
2. Add the mixed salad greens to the bowl and toss gently to combine all the ingredients.

3. In a small bowl, whisk together the ingredients for the dressing: extra virgin olive oil, lime juice, honey or maple syrup, ground cumin, chili powder, garlic powder, salt, and pepper.
4. Pour the dressing over the salad and toss gently to coat all ingredients evenly.
5. Divide the salad among serving plates or bowls.
6. Optional: top each serving with sliced jalapeños, diced avocado, shredded cheese, or tortilla strips for extra flavor and texture.
7. Serve the Southwest Black Bean and Chicken Salad immediately and enjoy this delicious and nutritious meal!

Feel free to customize your Southwest Black Bean and Chicken Salad by adding other ingredients such as diced mango, sliced black olives, or cooked quinoa. You can also adjust the dressing to suit your taste preferences by adding more or less lime juice, honey, cumin, or chili powder.

Asian-Inspired Beef and Noodle Salad

Ingredients:

For the Beef:

- 1 lb (450g) flank steak or sirloin steak
- 2 tablespoons soy sauce
- 2 tablespoons hoisin sauce
- 2 cloves garlic, minced
- 1 teaspoon grated ginger
- 1 tablespoon sesame oil
- Salt and pepper to taste

For the Salad:

- 8 oz (225g) rice noodles or soba noodles
- 4 cups mixed salad greens (such as baby spinach, arugula, and shredded cabbage)
- 1 cucumber, julienned
- 1 carrot, julienned
- 1 bell pepper (any color), thinly sliced
- 1/4 cup chopped fresh cilantro
- 1/4 cup chopped roasted peanuts or cashews
- Optional toppings: sliced green onions, sesame seeds, lime wedges

For the Dressing:

- 1/4 cup soy sauce
- 2 tablespoons rice vinegar
- 1 tablespoon honey or maple syrup
- 1 tablespoon sesame oil
- 1 teaspoon grated ginger
- 1 clove garlic, minced
- 1 teaspoon Sriracha or chili paste (optional, for heat)
- Salt and pepper to taste

Instructions:

1. In a small bowl, whisk together the soy sauce, hoisin sauce, minced garlic, grated ginger, sesame oil, salt, and pepper. Place the steak in a shallow dish or resealable plastic bag and pour the marinade over the steak. Marinate for at least 30 minutes, or up to 4 hours, in the refrigerator.
2. Cook the rice noodles or soba noodles according to the package instructions. Drain and rinse under cold water to stop the cooking process. Set aside.
3. Preheat a grill or grill pan over medium-high heat. Remove the steak from the marinade and discard the excess marinade. Grill the steak for about 4-5 minutes per side, or until it reaches your desired level of doneness. Remove from the grill and let it rest for a few minutes before slicing thinly against the grain.
4. In a large salad bowl, combine the cooked noodles, mixed salad greens, julienned cucumber, julienned carrot, thinly sliced bell pepper, and chopped fresh cilantro.
5. In a small bowl, whisk together the ingredients for the dressing: soy sauce, rice vinegar, honey or maple syrup, sesame oil, grated ginger, minced garlic, Sriracha or chili paste (if using), salt, and pepper.
6. Pour the dressing over the salad and toss gently to coat all ingredients evenly.
7. Divide the salad among serving plates or bowls.
8. Top each serving with slices of grilled steak and chopped roasted peanuts or cashews.
9. Optional: garnish with sliced green onions, sesame seeds, and lime wedges.
10. Serve the Asian-Inspired Beef and Noodle Salad immediately and enjoy this flavorful and satisfying meal!

Feel free to customize your Asian-Inspired Beef and Noodle Salad by adding other ingredients such as sliced mushrooms, bean sprouts, or snap peas. You can also adjust the dressing to suit your taste preferences by adding more or less honey, rice vinegar, or Sriracha.

Edamame and Brown Rice Salad with Tofu

Ingredients:

For the Salad:

- 1 cup brown rice, uncooked
- 1 1/2 cups shelled edamame (frozen or fresh)
- 1 block (14 oz) firm tofu, drained and cubed
- 1 red bell pepper, diced
- 1 carrot, grated
- 1/4 cup chopped green onions
- 1/4 cup chopped fresh cilantro
- 1/4 cup toasted sesame seeds
- Salt and pepper to taste

For the Dressing:

- 1/4 cup soy sauce or tamari
- 2 tablespoons rice vinegar
- 1 tablespoon sesame oil
- 1 tablespoon honey or maple syrup
- 1 teaspoon grated ginger
- 1 clove garlic, minced
- Red pepper flakes or Sriracha to taste (optional)

Instructions:

1. Cook the brown rice according to package instructions. Once cooked, let it cool to room temperature.
2. Cook the shelled edamame according to package instructions, if using frozen. Once cooked, rinse under cold water and drain.
3. In a large mixing bowl, combine the cooked brown rice, cooked edamame, cubed tofu, diced red bell pepper, grated carrot, chopped green onions, chopped fresh cilantro, and toasted sesame seeds. Season with salt and pepper to taste.

4. In a small bowl, whisk together the soy sauce or tamari, rice vinegar, sesame oil, honey or maple syrup, grated ginger, minced garlic, and red pepper flakes or Sriracha (if using).
5. Pour the dressing over the salad and toss gently to coat all ingredients evenly.
6. Serve the Edamame and Brown Rice Salad with Tofu immediately, or refrigerate for at least 30 minutes to allow the flavors to meld together.
7. Enjoy this nutritious and flavorful salad as a light and satisfying meal!

Feel free to customize your Edamame and Brown Rice Salad with Tofu by adding other ingredients such as sliced cucumber, shredded cabbage, or chopped avocado. You can also adjust the dressing to suit your taste preferences by adding more or less soy sauce, rice vinegar, or honey.

Chicken and Mango Salad with Coconut Dressing

Ingredients:

For the Salad:

- 2 boneless, skinless chicken breasts
- 1 ripe mango, peeled and diced
- 4 cups mixed salad greens (such as baby spinach, arugula, and romaine lettuce)
- 1/2 red bell pepper, thinly sliced
- 1/4 red onion, thinly sliced
- 1/4 cup chopped fresh cilantro
- 1/4 cup chopped roasted cashews or peanuts
- Optional: sliced avocado, shredded coconut for garnish

For the Coconut Dressing:

- 1/4 cup coconut milk
- 2 tablespoons lime juice
- 1 tablespoon honey or maple syrup
- 1 teaspoon soy sauce
- 1/2 teaspoon grated ginger
- Salt and pepper to taste

Instructions:

1. Preheat your grill or grill pan over medium-high heat.
2. Season the chicken breasts with salt and pepper. Grill the chicken for about 6-8 minutes per side, or until cooked through and no longer pink in the center. Remove from the grill and let it rest for a few minutes before slicing thinly.
3. In a large salad bowl, combine the diced mango, mixed salad greens, thinly sliced red bell pepper, thinly sliced red onion, chopped fresh cilantro, and chopped roasted cashews or peanuts. Add the sliced grilled chicken to the salad.
4. In a small bowl, whisk together the ingredients for the coconut dressing: coconut milk, lime juice, honey or maple syrup, soy sauce, grated ginger, salt, and pepper.

5. Pour the coconut dressing over the salad and toss gently to coat all ingredients evenly.
6. Divide the salad among serving plates or bowls.
7. Optional: garnish with sliced avocado and shredded coconut.
8. Serve the Chicken and Mango Salad with Coconut Dressing immediately and enjoy this tropical and flavorful dish!

Feel free to customize your Chicken and Mango Salad with Coconut Dressing by adding other ingredients such as cucumber slices, cherry tomatoes, or shredded carrots. You can also adjust the dressing to suit your taste preferences by adding more lime juice, honey, soy sauce, or ginger.

Mediterranean Orzo Salad with Grilled Chicken

Ingredients:

For the Grilled Chicken:

- 2 boneless, skinless chicken breasts
- 2 tablespoons olive oil
- 2 cloves garlic, minced
- 1 teaspoon dried oregano
- Salt and pepper to taste

For the Orzo Salad:

- 1 cup orzo pasta
- 1 cup cherry tomatoes, halved
- 1/2 cup cucumber, diced
- 1/4 cup red onion, finely chopped
- 1/4 cup Kalamata olives, pitted and halved
- 1/4 cup crumbled feta cheese
- 1/4 cup chopped fresh parsley
- 2 tablespoons chopped fresh mint
- 2 tablespoons extra virgin olive oil
- 2 tablespoons red wine vinegar
- 1 clove garlic, minced
- Salt and pepper to taste
- Optional: lemon wedges for serving

Instructions:

1. Preheat your grill or grill pan over medium-high heat.
2. In a small bowl, mix together olive oil, minced garlic, dried oregano, salt, and pepper. Coat the chicken breasts with the mixture on both sides.
3. Grill the chicken breasts for about 6-8 minutes per side, or until they are cooked through and no longer pink in the center. Once cooked, remove from the grill and let them rest for a few minutes before slicing.

4. Cook the orzo pasta according to package instructions. Drain and rinse under cold water to stop the cooking process. Transfer to a large mixing bowl.
5. Add the cherry tomatoes, diced cucumber, finely chopped red onion, halved Kalamata olives, crumbled feta cheese, chopped fresh parsley, and chopped fresh mint to the bowl with the cooked orzo pasta.
6. In a small bowl, whisk together the extra virgin olive oil, red wine vinegar, minced garlic, salt, and pepper. Pour the dressing over the orzo salad and toss gently to coat all ingredients evenly.
7. Divide the orzo salad among serving plates or bowls.
8. Top each serving with sliced grilled chicken.
9. Optional: serve with lemon wedges for squeezing over the chicken.
10. Serve the Mediterranean Orzo Salad with Grilled Chicken immediately and enjoy this flavorful and satisfying dish!

Feel free to customize your Mediterranean Orzo Salad with Grilled Chicken by adding other ingredients such as roasted red peppers, artichoke hearts, or pine nuts. You can also adjust the dressing to suit your taste preferences by adding more or less olive oil, red wine vinegar, garlic, or herbs.

Quinoa and Kale Salad with Lemon Herb Chicken

Ingredients:

For the Lemon Herb Chicken:

- 2 boneless, skinless chicken breasts
- 2 tablespoons olive oil
- Zest and juice of 1 lemon
- 2 cloves garlic, minced
- 1 teaspoon dried thyme
- 1 teaspoon dried rosemary
- Salt and pepper to taste

For the Quinoa and Kale Salad:

- 1 cup quinoa, rinsed
- 2 cups water or chicken broth
- 4 cups chopped kale leaves, tough stems removed
- 1/4 cup sliced almonds, toasted
- 1/4 cup dried cranberries or raisins
- 1/4 cup crumbled feta cheese or goat cheese
- Optional: sliced avocado for serving

For the Lemon Herb Dressing:

- 1/4 cup extra virgin olive oil
- Zest and juice of 1 lemon
- 1 tablespoon honey or maple syrup
- 1 teaspoon Dijon mustard
- 1 clove garlic, minced
- 1 teaspoon dried oregano
- Salt and pepper to taste

Instructions:

1. Preheat your grill or grill pan over medium-high heat.
2. In a small bowl, mix together olive oil, lemon zest, lemon juice, minced garlic, dried thyme, dried rosemary, salt, and pepper. Coat the chicken breasts with the mixture on both sides.
3. Grill the chicken breasts for about 6-8 minutes per side, or until they are cooked through and no longer pink in the center. Once cooked, remove from the grill and let them rest for a few minutes before slicing.
4. In a medium saucepan, combine the quinoa and water or chicken broth. Bring to a boil, then reduce the heat to low, cover, and simmer for 15-20 minutes, or until the quinoa is cooked and the liquid is absorbed. Remove from heat and let it sit, covered, for 5 minutes. Fluff with a fork and let it cool slightly.
5. In a large mixing bowl, massage the chopped kale leaves with a drizzle of olive oil for a few minutes until they become slightly tender and wilted.
6. Add the cooked quinoa, sliced almonds, dried cranberries or raisins, and crumbled feta cheese or goat cheese to the bowl with the massaged kale leaves. Toss gently to combine.
7. In a small bowl, whisk together the ingredients for the lemon herb dressing: extra virgin olive oil, lemon zest, lemon juice, honey or maple syrup, Dijon mustard, minced garlic, dried oregano, salt, and pepper.
8. Pour the lemon herb dressing over the quinoa and kale salad and toss gently to coat all ingredients evenly.
9. Divide the salad among serving plates or bowls.
10. Top each serving with sliced grilled chicken.
11. Optional: serve with sliced avocado on the side.
12. Serve the Quinoa and Kale Salad with Lemon Herb Chicken immediately and enjoy this flavorful and nutritious meal!

Feel free to customize your Quinoa and Kale Salad with Lemon Herb Chicken by adding other ingredients such as cherry tomatoes, cucumber slices, or roasted vegetables. You can also adjust the dressing to suit your taste preferences by adding more or less lemon juice, honey, Dijon mustard, or herbs.

Tofu and Avocado Salad with Miso Dressing

Ingredients:

For the Tofu:

- 1 block (14 oz) firm tofu, drained and pressed
- 2 tablespoons soy sauce
- 1 tablespoon sesame oil
- 1 teaspoon grated ginger
- 2 cloves garlic, minced
- Salt and pepper to taste

For the Salad:

- 4 cups mixed salad greens (such as baby spinach, arugula, and romaine lettuce)
- 1 avocado, sliced
- 1/4 cup sliced cucumber
- 1/4 cup shredded carrots
- 1/4 cup sliced radishes
- 2 green onions, thinly sliced
- 2 tablespoons chopped fresh cilantro or parsley
- Optional: sesame seeds or chopped roasted peanuts for garnish

For the Miso Dressing:

- 2 tablespoons white miso paste
- 2 tablespoons rice vinegar
- 1 tablespoon soy sauce
- 1 tablespoon sesame oil
- 1 tablespoon honey or maple syrup
- 1 teaspoon grated ginger
- 1 clove garlic, minced
- 2 tablespoons water (or more as needed to thin the dressing)
- Salt and pepper to taste

Instructions:

1. Preheat your grill or grill pan over medium-high heat.
2. Slice the pressed tofu into cubes or rectangles, depending on your preference.
3. In a shallow dish, whisk together soy sauce, sesame oil, grated ginger, minced garlic, salt, and pepper. Place the tofu cubes in the marinade, ensuring they are evenly coated. Let them marinate for about 15-20 minutes.
4. Grill the marinated tofu for about 4-5 minutes per side, or until lightly charred and heated through. Remove from the grill and set aside.
5. In a large salad bowl, combine the mixed salad greens, sliced avocado, sliced cucumber, shredded carrots, sliced radishes, sliced green onions, and chopped fresh cilantro or parsley.
6. In a small bowl, whisk together the ingredients for the miso dressing: white miso paste, rice vinegar, soy sauce, sesame oil, honey or maple syrup, grated ginger, minced garlic, water, salt, and pepper. Adjust the consistency by adding more water if needed to thin the dressing.
7. Drizzle the miso dressing over the salad and toss gently to coat all ingredients evenly.
8. Divide the salad among serving plates or bowls.
9. Top each serving with grilled tofu cubes.
10. Optional: garnish with sesame seeds or chopped roasted peanuts.
11. Serve the Tofu and Avocado Salad with Miso Dressing immediately and enjoy this flavorful and nutritious meal!

Feel free to customize your Tofu and Avocado Salad with Miso Dressing by adding other ingredients such as cherry tomatoes, bell peppers, or edamame. You can also adjust the dressing to suit your taste preferences by adding more or less soy sauce, rice vinegar, honey, or ginger.

Grilled Shrimp and Pineapple Salad

Ingredients:

For the Grilled Shrimp:

- 1 lb (450g) large shrimp, peeled and deveined
- 2 tablespoons olive oil
- 2 cloves garlic, minced
- Zest and juice of 1 lime
- 1 teaspoon paprika
- Salt and pepper to taste

For the Salad:

- 1 small pineapple, peeled, cored, and cut into chunks
- 4 cups mixed salad greens (such as baby spinach, arugula, and romaine lettuce)
- 1/4 cup red onion, thinly sliced
- 1/4 cup chopped fresh cilantro
- 1/4 cup chopped roasted cashews or peanuts
- Optional: sliced avocado for serving

For the Dressing:

- 1/4 cup extra virgin olive oil
- 2 tablespoons rice vinegar
- Zest and juice of 1 lime
- 1 tablespoon honey or maple syrup
- 1 teaspoon grated ginger
- 1 clove garlic, minced
- Salt and pepper to taste

Instructions:

1. Preheat your grill or grill pan over medium-high heat.
2. In a shallow dish, whisk together olive oil, minced garlic, lime zest, lime juice, paprika, salt, and pepper. Add the peeled and deveined shrimp to the marinade, ensuring they are evenly coated. Let them marinate for about 15-20 minutes.
3. Thread the pineapple chunks onto skewers. Grill the pineapple skewers for about 3-4 minutes per side, or until they are lightly charred and caramelized. Remove from the grill and set aside.
4. Grill the marinated shrimp for about 2-3 minutes per side, or until they are pink and opaque. Remove from the grill and set aside.
5. In a large salad bowl, combine the mixed salad greens, thinly sliced red onion, chopped fresh cilantro, and chopped roasted cashews or peanuts.
6. In a small bowl, whisk together the ingredients for the dressing: extra virgin olive oil, rice vinegar, lime zest, lime juice, honey or maple syrup, grated ginger, minced garlic, salt, and pepper.
7. Drizzle the dressing over the salad and toss gently to coat all ingredients evenly.
8. Divide the salad among serving plates or bowls.
9. Top each serving with grilled shrimp and grilled pineapple chunks.
10. Optional: serve with sliced avocado on the side.
11. Serve the Grilled Shrimp and Pineapple Salad immediately and enjoy this tropical and flavorful dish!

Feel free to customize your Grilled Shrimp and Pineapple Salad by adding other ingredients such as cherry tomatoes, cucumber slices, or shredded carrots. You can also adjust the dressing to suit your taste preferences by adding more or less lime juice, honey, or ginger.

Spinach and Strawberry Salad with Grilled Chicken

Ingredients:

For the Grilled Chicken:

- 2 boneless, skinless chicken breasts
- 2 tablespoons olive oil
- Zest and juice of 1 lemon
- 2 cloves garlic, minced
- 1 teaspoon dried oregano
- Salt and pepper to taste

For the Salad:

- 6 cups baby spinach leaves
- 2 cups sliced strawberries
- 1/4 cup sliced red onion
- 1/4 cup crumbled feta cheese or goat cheese
- 1/4 cup chopped walnuts or pecans, toasted
- Optional: sliced avocado for serving

For the Balsamic Vinaigrette:

- 1/4 cup balsamic vinegar
- 1/4 cup extra virgin olive oil
- 1 tablespoon honey or maple syrup
- 1 teaspoon Dijon mustard
- Salt and pepper to taste

Instructions:

1. Preheat your grill or grill pan over medium-high heat.

2. In a shallow dish, whisk together olive oil, lemon zest, lemon juice, minced garlic, dried oregano, salt, and pepper. Add the chicken breasts to the marinade, ensuring they are evenly coated. Let them marinate for about 15-20 minutes.
3. Grill the marinated chicken breasts for about 6-8 minutes per side, or until they are cooked through and no longer pink in the center. Once cooked, remove from the grill and let them rest for a few minutes before slicing.
4. In a large salad bowl, combine the baby spinach leaves, sliced strawberries, sliced red onion, crumbled feta cheese or goat cheese, and chopped toasted walnuts or pecans.
5. In a small bowl, whisk together the ingredients for the balsamic vinaigrette: balsamic vinegar, extra virgin olive oil, honey or maple syrup, Dijon mustard, salt, and pepper.
6. Drizzle the balsamic vinaigrette over the salad and toss gently to coat all ingredients evenly.
7. Divide the salad among serving plates or bowls.
8. Top each serving with sliced grilled chicken.
9. Optional: serve with sliced avocado on the side.
10. Serve the Spinach and Strawberry Salad with Grilled Chicken immediately and enjoy this delicious and nutritious meal!

Feel free to customize your Spinach and Strawberry Salad with Grilled Chicken by adding other ingredients such as sliced almonds, crumbled bacon, or dried cranberries. You can also adjust the dressing to suit your taste preferences by adding more or less honey, Dijon mustard, or balsamic vinegar.

Greek Pasta Salad with Turkey Sausage

Ingredients:

For the Turkey Sausage:

- 1 lb (450g) turkey sausage, casings removed
- 1 tablespoon olive oil
- 1 teaspoon dried oregano
- 1 teaspoon dried basil
- 1/2 teaspoon garlic powder
- Salt and pepper to taste

For the Pasta Salad:

- 8 oz (225g) rotini or fusilli pasta
- 1 cup cherry tomatoes, halved
- 1 cucumber, diced
- 1/2 red onion, thinly sliced
- 1/2 cup sliced Kalamata olives
- 1/2 cup crumbled feta cheese
- 1/4 cup chopped fresh parsley
- Optional: sliced pepperoncini peppers for garnish

For the Greek Dressing:

- 1/4 cup extra virgin olive oil
- 2 tablespoons red wine vinegar
- 1 teaspoon dried oregano
- 1 clove garlic, minced
- Salt and pepper to taste

Instructions:

1. Cook the pasta according to package instructions until al dente. Drain and rinse under cold water to stop the cooking process. Set aside.
2. In a large skillet, heat olive oil over medium heat. Add the turkey sausage, breaking it apart with a wooden spoon, and cook until browned and cooked through, about 8-10 minutes. Stir in dried oregano, dried basil, garlic powder, salt, and pepper. Remove from heat and set aside.
3. In a large mixing bowl, combine the cooked pasta, halved cherry tomatoes, diced cucumber, thinly sliced red onion, sliced Kalamata olives, crumbled feta cheese, and chopped fresh parsley.
4. In a small bowl, whisk together the ingredients for the Greek dressing: extra virgin olive oil, red wine vinegar, dried oregano, minced garlic, salt, and pepper.
5. Pour the Greek dressing over the pasta salad and toss gently to coat all ingredients evenly.
6. Add the cooked turkey sausage to the pasta salad and toss again to combine.
7. Divide the pasta salad among serving plates or bowls.
8. Optional: garnish with sliced pepperoncini peppers for extra flavor and a pop of color.
9. Serve the Greek Pasta Salad with Turkey Sausage immediately and enjoy this flavorful and satisfying dish!

Feel free to customize your Greek Pasta Salad with Turkey Sausage by adding other ingredients such as diced bell peppers, artichoke hearts, or chopped spinach. You can also adjust the dressing to suit your taste preferences by adding more or less red wine vinegar, garlic, or herbs.

Roasted Vegetable and Chickpea Salad with Quinoa

Ingredients:

For the Roasted Vegetables and Chickpeas:

- 1 large sweet potato, peeled and diced
- 1 large red bell pepper, diced
- 1 large zucchini, diced
- 1 can (15 oz) chickpeas, drained and rinsed
- 2 tablespoons olive oil
- 1 teaspoon ground cumin
- 1 teaspoon paprika
- 1/2 teaspoon garlic powder
- Salt and pepper to taste

For the Quinoa:

- 1 cup quinoa, rinsed
- 2 cups water or vegetable broth

For the Salad:

- 4 cups baby spinach or mixed salad greens
- 1/4 cup chopped fresh parsley
- 1/4 cup crumbled feta cheese or goat cheese
- 1/4 cup toasted pumpkin seeds or sunflower seeds

For the Dressing:

- 1/4 cup extra virgin olive oil
- 2 tablespoons balsamic vinegar
- 1 tablespoon honey or maple syrup
- 1 teaspoon Dijon mustard

- Salt and pepper to taste

Instructions:

1. Preheat your oven to 400°F (200°C).
2. In a large mixing bowl, combine the diced sweet potato, diced red bell pepper, diced zucchini, and drained and rinsed chickpeas.
3. Drizzle the olive oil over the vegetables and chickpeas. Sprinkle with ground cumin, paprika, garlic powder, salt, and pepper. Toss gently to coat all ingredients evenly.
4. Spread the seasoned vegetables and chickpeas in a single layer on a large baking sheet lined with parchment paper.
5. Roast in the preheated oven for 25-30 minutes, or until the vegetables are tender and lightly browned, stirring halfway through the cooking time.
6. While the vegetables and chickpeas are roasting, cook the quinoa. In a medium saucepan, combine the rinsed quinoa and water or vegetable broth. Bring to a boil, then reduce the heat to low, cover, and simmer for 15-20 minutes, or until the quinoa is cooked and the liquid is absorbed. Remove from heat and let it sit, covered, for 5 minutes. Fluff with a fork and let it cool slightly.
7. In a large salad bowl, combine the cooked quinoa, roasted vegetables, chickpeas, baby spinach or mixed salad greens, chopped fresh parsley, crumbled feta cheese or goat cheese, and toasted pumpkin seeds or sunflower seeds.
8. In a small bowl, whisk together the ingredients for the dressing: extra virgin olive oil, balsamic vinegar, honey or maple syrup, Dijon mustard, salt, and pepper.
9. Drizzle the dressing over the salad and toss gently to coat all ingredients evenly.
10. Divide the salad among serving plates or bowls.
11. Serve the Roasted Vegetable and Chickpea Salad with Quinoa immediately and enjoy this flavorful and nutritious dish!

Feel free to customize your Roasted Vegetable and Chickpea Salad with Quinoa by adding other roasted vegetables such as cauliflower, broccoli, or carrots. You can also adjust the dressing to suit your taste preferences by adding more or less balsamic vinegar, honey, or Dijon mustard.

Thai Beef Salad with Peanut Dressing

Ingredients:

For the Beef:

- 1 lb (450g) beef sirloin or flank steak
- 2 tablespoons soy sauce
- 1 tablespoon fish sauce
- 1 tablespoon lime juice
- 2 cloves garlic, minced
- 1 teaspoon grated ginger
- 1 teaspoon brown sugar
- Salt and pepper to taste

For the Salad:

- 6 cups mixed salad greens (such as lettuce, spinach, and arugula)
- 1 cucumber, thinly sliced
- 1 carrot, julienned or grated
- 1/2 red bell pepper, thinly sliced
- 1/4 cup chopped fresh cilantro
- 1/4 cup chopped fresh mint
- 1/4 cup chopped roasted peanuts
- Optional: sliced red chili for garnish

For the Peanut Dressing:

- 1/4 cup creamy peanut butter
- 2 tablespoons soy sauce
- 1 tablespoon rice vinegar
- 1 tablespoon honey or maple syrup
- 1 tablespoon sesame oil
- 1 clove garlic, minced
- 1 teaspoon grated ginger
- Water (as needed to thin the dressing)

- Salt and pepper to taste

Instructions:

1. In a small bowl, whisk together soy sauce, fish sauce, lime juice, minced garlic, grated ginger, brown sugar, salt, and pepper. Place the beef in a shallow dish and pour the marinade over it. Let it marinate for at least 30 minutes, or up to 2 hours in the refrigerator.
2. Preheat your grill or grill pan over medium-high heat. Remove the beef from the marinade and discard any excess marinade. Grill the beef for about 4-5 minutes per side, or until cooked to your desired doneness. Once cooked, remove from the grill and let it rest for a few minutes before slicing thinly against the grain.
3. In a large salad bowl, combine the mixed salad greens, thinly sliced cucumber, julienned or grated carrot, thinly sliced red bell pepper, chopped fresh cilantro, and chopped fresh mint.
4. In a small bowl, whisk together the ingredients for the peanut dressing: creamy peanut butter, soy sauce, rice vinegar, honey or maple syrup, sesame oil, minced garlic, grated ginger, and water (as needed to achieve your desired consistency). Season with salt and pepper to taste.
5. Drizzle the peanut dressing over the salad and toss gently to coat all ingredients evenly.
6. Divide the salad among serving plates or bowls.
7. Top each serving with sliced grilled beef and chopped roasted peanuts.
8. Optional: garnish with sliced red chili for extra heat and color.
9. Serve the Thai Beef Salad with Peanut Dressing immediately and enjoy this flavorful and satisfying dish!

Feel free to customize your Thai Beef Salad with Peanut Dressing by adding other ingredients such as bean sprouts, sliced red onion, or cooked rice noodles. You can also adjust the dressing to suit your taste preferences by adding more or less soy sauce, honey, or ginger.

Chicken Caesar Pasta Salad

Ingredients:

For the Chicken:

- 2 boneless, skinless chicken breasts
- 2 tablespoons olive oil
- 1 teaspoon garlic powder
- 1 teaspoon dried oregano
- Salt and pepper to taste

For the Pasta Salad:

- 8 oz (225g) penne pasta
- 4 cups chopped romaine lettuce
- 1 cup cherry tomatoes, halved
- 1/4 cup sliced black olives
- 1/4 cup grated Parmesan cheese
- Optional: croutons for serving

For the Caesar Dressing:

- 1/2 cup mayonnaise
- 1/4 cup grated Parmesan cheese
- 2 tablespoons lemon juice
- 1 tablespoon Dijon mustard
- 1 teaspoon Worcestershire sauce
- 1 clove garlic, minced
- Salt and pepper to taste

Instructions:

1. Preheat your grill or grill pan over medium-high heat.

2. Season the chicken breasts with olive oil, garlic powder, dried oregano, salt, and pepper. Grill the chicken for about 6-8 minutes per side, or until cooked through and no longer pink in the center. Once cooked, remove from the grill and let them rest for a few minutes before slicing.
3. Cook the penne pasta according to package instructions until al dente. Drain and rinse under cold water to stop the cooking process. Let it cool slightly.
4. In a large mixing bowl, combine the cooked penne pasta, chopped romaine lettuce, halved cherry tomatoes, sliced black olives, and grated Parmesan cheese.
5. In a small bowl, whisk together the ingredients for the Caesar dressing: mayonnaise, grated Parmesan cheese, lemon juice, Dijon mustard, Worcestershire sauce, minced garlic, salt, and pepper.
6. Pour the Caesar dressing over the pasta salad and toss gently to coat all ingredients evenly.
7. Divide the pasta salad among serving plates or bowls.
8. Top each serving with sliced grilled chicken.
9. Optional: garnish with croutons for added crunch.
10. Serve the Chicken Caesar Pasta Salad immediately and enjoy this flavorful and satisfying dish!

Feel free to customize your Chicken Caesar Pasta Salad by adding other ingredients such as bacon bits, sliced red onion, or diced avocado. You can also adjust the dressing to suit your taste preferences by adding more or less lemon juice, Dijon mustard, or Parmesan cheese.

Blackened Salmon and Mango Salad

Ingredients:

For the Blackened Salmon:

- 2 salmon fillets (about 6 oz each), skin-on
- 2 tablespoons olive oil
- 1 tablespoon paprika
- 1 teaspoon garlic powder
- 1 teaspoon onion powder
- 1 teaspoon dried thyme
- 1/2 teaspoon cayenne pepper (adjust to taste)
- Salt and pepper to taste

For the Salad:

- 4 cups mixed salad greens (such as baby spinach, arugula, and romaine lettuce)
- 1 ripe mango, peeled, pitted, and diced
- 1/4 cup thinly sliced red onion
- 1/4 cup chopped fresh cilantro
- 1/4 cup chopped roasted almonds or cashews

For the Lime Dressing:

- 1/4 cup extra virgin olive oil
- Zest and juice of 1 lime
- 1 tablespoon honey or maple syrup
- 1 teaspoon Dijon mustard
- 1 clove garlic, minced
- Salt and pepper to taste

Instructions:

1. Preheat your grill or grill pan over medium-high heat.
2. In a small bowl, mix together olive oil, paprika, garlic powder, onion powder, dried thyme, cayenne pepper, salt, and pepper. Brush the mixture over the salmon fillets, coating them evenly.
3. Place the salmon fillets skin-side down on the preheated grill or grill pan. Cook for about 4-5 minutes on each side, or until the salmon is cooked through and flakes easily with a fork. Once cooked, remove from the grill and let them rest for a few minutes.
4. In a large salad bowl, combine the mixed salad greens, diced mango, thinly sliced red onion, chopped fresh cilantro, and chopped roasted almonds or cashews.
5. In a small bowl, whisk together the ingredients for the lime dressing: extra virgin olive oil, lime zest, lime juice, honey or maple syrup, Dijon mustard, minced garlic, salt, and pepper.
6. Drizzle the lime dressing over the salad and toss gently to coat all ingredients evenly.
7. Divide the salad among serving plates or bowls.
8. Top each serving with a grilled salmon fillet.
9. Serve the Blackened Salmon and Mango Salad immediately and enjoy this flavorful and nutritious dish!

Feel free to customize your Blackened Salmon and Mango Salad by adding other ingredients such as sliced avocado, cherry tomatoes, or cucumber. You can also adjust the dressing to suit your taste preferences by adding more or less lime juice, honey, or Dijon mustard.

Lentil and Kale Salad with Grilled Chicken

Ingredients:

For the Grilled Chicken:

- 2 boneless, skinless chicken breasts
- 2 tablespoons olive oil
- 1 teaspoon dried oregano
- 1 teaspoon dried thyme
- Salt and pepper to taste

For the Lentil and Kale Salad:

- 1 cup green lentils, rinsed
- 3 cups water or vegetable broth
- 4 cups chopped kale leaves, tough stems removed
- 1/4 cup diced red onion
- 1/4 cup chopped fresh parsley
- 1/4 cup chopped roasted almonds or walnuts
- Optional: sliced avocado for serving

For the Lemon Herb Dressing:

- 1/4 cup extra virgin olive oil
- Zest and juice of 1 lemon
- 1 tablespoon honey or maple syrup
- 1 teaspoon Dijon mustard
- 1 clove garlic, minced
- 1 teaspoon dried oregano
- Salt and pepper to taste

Instructions:

1. Preheat your grill or grill pan over medium-high heat.
2. In a small bowl, whisk together olive oil, dried oregano, dried thyme, salt, and pepper. Coat the chicken breasts with the mixture on both sides.
3. Grill the chicken breasts for about 6-8 minutes per side, or until they are cooked through and no longer pink in the center. Once cooked, remove from the grill and let them rest for a few minutes before slicing.
4. In a medium saucepan, combine the green lentils and water or vegetable broth. Bring to a boil, then reduce the heat to low, cover, and simmer for 15-20 minutes, or until the lentils are tender but still hold their shape. Drain any excess liquid and let the lentils cool slightly.
5. In a large mixing bowl, massage the chopped kale leaves with a drizzle of olive oil for a few minutes until they become slightly tender and wilted.
6. Add the cooked lentils, diced red onion, chopped fresh parsley, and chopped roasted almonds or walnuts to the bowl with the massaged kale leaves. Toss gently to combine.
7. In a small bowl, whisk together the ingredients for the lemon herb dressing: extra virgin olive oil, lemon zest, lemon juice, honey or maple syrup, Dijon mustard, minced garlic, dried oregano, salt, and pepper.
8. Pour the lemon herb dressing over the lentil and kale salad and toss gently to coat all ingredients evenly.
9. Divide the salad among serving plates or bowls.
10. Top each serving with sliced grilled chicken.
11. Optional: serve with sliced avocado on the side.
12. Serve the Lentil and Kale Salad with Grilled Chicken immediately and enjoy this flavorful and nutritious meal!

Feel free to customize your Lentil and Kale Salad with Grilled Chicken by adding other ingredients such as cherry tomatoes, cucumber slices, or crumbled feta cheese. You can also adjust the dressing to suit your taste preferences by adding more or less lemon juice, honey, or Dijon mustard.

Quinoa and Black Bean Salad with Avocado

Ingredients:

For the Salad:

- 1 cup quinoa, rinsed
- 2 cups water or vegetable broth
- 1 can (15 oz) black beans, drained and rinsed
- 1 red bell pepper, diced
- 1/2 cup diced red onion
- 1/4 cup chopped fresh cilantro
- 1 avocado, diced
- Optional: sliced jalapeno for garnish

For the Dressing:

- 1/4 cup lime juice (about 2-3 limes)
- 2 tablespoons extra virgin olive oil
- 1 teaspoon ground cumin
- 1/2 teaspoon chili powder
- 1/4 teaspoon garlic powder
- Salt and pepper to taste

Instructions:

1. In a medium saucepan, combine the quinoa and water or vegetable broth. Bring to a boil, then reduce the heat to low, cover, and simmer for 15-20 minutes, or until the quinoa is cooked and the liquid is absorbed. Remove from heat and let it sit, covered, for 5 minutes. Fluff with a fork and let it cool slightly.
2. In a large mixing bowl, combine the cooked quinoa, black beans, diced red bell pepper, diced red onion, chopped fresh cilantro, and diced avocado.
3. In a small bowl, whisk together the ingredients for the dressing: lime juice, extra virgin olive oil, ground cumin, chili powder, garlic powder, salt, and pepper.
4. Pour the dressing over the salad and toss gently to coat all ingredients evenly.
5. Divide the salad among serving plates or bowls.

6. Optional: garnish with sliced jalapeno for extra heat and flavor.
7. Serve the Quinoa and Black Bean Salad with Avocado immediately and enjoy this flavorful and nutritious dish!

Feel free to customize your Quinoa and Black Bean Salad with Avocado by adding other ingredients such as corn kernels, cherry tomatoes, or chopped green onions. You can also adjust the dressing to suit your taste preferences by adding more or less lime juice, cumin, or chili powder.

Spinach and Goat Cheese Salad with Grilled Steak

Ingredients:

For the Grilled Steak:

- 2 beef sirloin steaks (about 6 oz each)
- 2 tablespoons olive oil
- 2 cloves garlic, minced
- 1 teaspoon dried thyme
- Salt and pepper to taste

For the Salad:

- 6 cups baby spinach leaves
- 1/2 cup cherry tomatoes, halved
- 1/4 cup thinly sliced red onion
- 1/4 cup toasted walnuts or pecans
- 1/4 cup crumbled goat cheese

For the Balsamic Vinaigrette:

- 1/4 cup balsamic vinegar
- 1/4 cup extra virgin olive oil
- 1 tablespoon honey or maple syrup
- 1 teaspoon Dijon mustard
- Salt and pepper to taste

Instructions:

1. Preheat your grill or grill pan over medium-high heat.
2. In a small bowl, whisk together olive oil, minced garlic, dried thyme, salt, and pepper. Rub the mixture over the steak on both sides.
3. Grill the steaks for about 4-5 minutes per side, or until they reach your desired level of doneness. Once cooked, remove from the grill and let them rest for a few minutes before slicing thinly against the grain.

4. In a large salad bowl, combine the baby spinach leaves, halved cherry tomatoes, thinly sliced red onion, toasted walnuts or pecans, and crumbled goat cheese.
5. In a small bowl, whisk together the ingredients for the balsamic vinaigrette: balsamic vinegar, extra virgin olive oil, honey or maple syrup, Dijon mustard, salt, and pepper.
6. Drizzle the balsamic vinaigrette over the salad and toss gently to coat all ingredients evenly.
7. Divide the salad among serving plates or bowls.
8. Top each serving with sliced grilled steak.
9. Serve the Spinach and Goat Cheese Salad with Grilled Steak immediately and enjoy this flavorful and satisfying dish!

Feel free to customize your Spinach and Goat Cheese Salad with Grilled Steak by adding other ingredients such as sliced avocado, cucumber slices, or crumbled bacon. You can also adjust the dressing to suit your taste preferences by adding more or less balsamic vinegar, honey, or Dijon mustard.

Chicken and Broccoli Salad with Sesame Dressing

Ingredients:

For the Grilled Steak:

- 2 beef sirloin steaks (about 6 oz each)
- 2 tablespoons olive oil
- 2 cloves garlic, minced
- 1 teaspoon dried thyme
- Salt and pepper to taste

For the Salad:

- 6 cups baby spinach leaves
- 1/2 cup cherry tomatoes, halved
- 1/4 cup thinly sliced red onion
- 1/4 cup toasted walnuts or pecans
- 1/4 cup crumbled goat cheese

For the Balsamic Vinaigrette:

- 1/4 cup balsamic vinegar
- 1/4 cup extra virgin olive oil
- 1 tablespoon honey or maple syrup
- 1 teaspoon Dijon mustard
- Salt and pepper to taste

Instructions:

1. Preheat your grill or grill pan over medium-high heat.
2. In a small bowl, whisk together olive oil, minced garlic, dried thyme, salt, and pepper. Rub the mixture over the steak on both sides.

3. Grill the steaks for about 4-5 minutes per side, or until they reach your desired level of doneness. Once cooked, remove from the grill and let them rest for a few minutes before slicing thinly against the grain.
4. In a large salad bowl, combine the baby spinach leaves, halved cherry tomatoes, thinly sliced red onion, toasted walnuts or pecans, and crumbled goat cheese.
5. In a small bowl, whisk together the ingredients for the balsamic vinaigrette: balsamic vinegar, extra virgin olive oil, honey or maple syrup, Dijon mustard, salt, and pepper.
6. Drizzle the balsamic vinaigrette over the salad and toss gently to coat all ingredients evenly.
7. Divide the salad among serving plates or bowls.
8. Top each serving with sliced grilled steak.
9. Serve the Spinach and Goat Cheese Salad with Grilled Steak immediately and enjoy this flavorful and satisfying dish!

Feel free to customize your Spinach and Goat Cheese Salad with Grilled Steak by adding other ingredients such as sliced avocado, cucumber slices, or crumbled bacon. You can also adjust the dressing to suit your taste preferences by adding more or less balsamic vinegar, honey, or Dijon mustard.

Chicken and Broccoli Salad with Sesame Dressing

Here's a delicious recipe for Chicken and Broccoli Salad with Sesame Dressing:

Ingredients:

For the Chicken:

- 2 boneless, skinless chicken breasts
- 2 tablespoons soy sauce
- 1 tablespoon sesame oil
- 1 tablespoon honey
- 2 cloves garlic, minced
- Salt and pepper to taste

For the Broccoli:

- 2 cups broccoli florets
- 1 tablespoon olive oil
- Salt and pepper to taste

For the Salad:

- 4 cups mixed salad greens (such as lettuce, spinach, and arugula)
- 1/2 cup shredded carrots
- 1/4 cup sliced red bell pepper
- 1/4 cup sliced cucumber
- 2 green onions, thinly sliced
- 1/4 cup chopped fresh cilantro or parsley
- Optional: toasted sesame seeds for garnish

For the Sesame Dressing:

- 2 tablespoons soy sauce
- 2 tablespoons rice vinegar

- 1 tablespoon sesame oil
- 1 tablespoon honey
- 1 teaspoon grated ginger
- 1 clove garlic, minced
- Salt and pepper to taste

Instructions:

1. Preheat your grill or grill pan over medium-high heat.
2. In a small bowl, whisk together soy sauce, sesame oil, honey, minced garlic, salt, and pepper. Coat the chicken breasts with the mixture on both sides.
3. Grill the chicken breasts for about 6-8 minutes per side, or until they are cooked through and no longer pink in the center. Once cooked, remove from the grill and let them rest for a few minutes before slicing thinly.
4. In a large mixing bowl, toss the broccoli florets with olive oil, salt, and pepper. Spread them in a single layer on a baking sheet lined with parchment paper. Roast in a preheated oven at 400°F (200°C) for 15-20 minutes, or until the broccoli is tender and slightly browned.
5. In a large salad bowl, combine the mixed salad greens, shredded carrots, sliced red bell pepper, sliced cucumber, thinly sliced green onions, and chopped fresh cilantro or parsley.
6. In a small bowl, whisk together the ingredients for the sesame dressing: soy sauce, rice vinegar, sesame oil, honey, grated ginger, minced garlic, salt, and pepper.
7. Drizzle the sesame dressing over the salad and toss gently to coat all ingredients evenly.
8. Divide the salad among serving plates or bowls.
9. Top each serving with sliced grilled chicken and roasted broccoli.
10. Optional: sprinkle with toasted sesame seeds for added flavor and crunch.
11. Serve the Chicken and Broccoli Salad with Sesame Dressing immediately and enjoy this flavorful and nutritious dish!

Feel free to customize your Chicken and Broccoli Salad with Sesame Dressing by adding other ingredients such as sliced avocado, edamame beans, or mandarin orange segments. You can also adjust the dressing to suit your taste preferences by adding more or less honey, sesame oil, or ginger.

Roasted Cauliflower and Chickpea Salad with Tofu

Ingredients:

For the Roasted Cauliflower and Chickpeas:

- 1 head cauliflower, cut into florets
- 1 can (15 oz) chickpeas, drained and rinsed
- 2 tablespoons olive oil
- 1 teaspoon ground cumin
- 1 teaspoon smoked paprika
- 1/2 teaspoon garlic powder
- Salt and pepper to taste

For the Tofu:

- 1 block (14 oz) firm tofu, drained and pressed
- 2 tablespoons soy sauce
- 1 tablespoon maple syrup or honey
- 1 tablespoon sesame oil
- 1 teaspoon grated ginger
- 1 clove garlic, minced
- Salt and pepper to taste

For the Salad:

- 4 cups mixed salad greens (such as lettuce, spinach, and arugula)
- 1/2 cup sliced cucumber
- 1/2 cup halved cherry tomatoes
- 1/4 cup sliced red onion
- 1/4 cup chopped fresh cilantro or parsley
- Optional: toasted sesame seeds for garnish

For the Tahini Dressing:

- 1/4 cup tahini
- 2 tablespoons lemon juice
- 1 tablespoon olive oil
- 1 tablespoon water (or more as needed for desired consistency)
- 1 teaspoon maple syrup or honey
- 1 clove garlic, minced
- Salt and pepper to taste

Instructions:

1. Preheat your oven to 425°F (220°C).
2. In a large mixing bowl, toss the cauliflower florets and chickpeas with olive oil, ground cumin, smoked paprika, garlic powder, salt, and pepper until evenly coated.
3. Spread the seasoned cauliflower and chickpeas in a single layer on a baking sheet lined with parchment paper. Roast in the preheated oven for 25-30 minutes, or until the cauliflower is tender and lightly browned, stirring halfway through the cooking time.
4. While the cauliflower and chickpeas are roasting, prepare the tofu. Cut the pressed tofu into cubes and place them in a shallow dish. In a small bowl, whisk together soy sauce, maple syrup or honey, sesame oil, grated ginger, minced garlic, salt, and pepper. Pour the marinade over the tofu cubes, coating them evenly. Let them marinate for about 15 minutes.
5. Heat a skillet over medium-high heat. Add the marinated tofu cubes (reserving any excess marinade) and cook for 4-5 minutes per side, or until the tofu is golden brown and crispy on the outside. Remove from heat and set aside.
6. In a large salad bowl, combine the mixed salad greens, sliced cucumber, halved cherry tomatoes, sliced red onion, and chopped fresh cilantro or parsley.
7. In a small bowl, whisk together the ingredients for the tahini dressing: tahini, lemon juice, olive oil, water, maple syrup or honey, minced garlic, salt, and pepper. Adjust the consistency with more water if needed.
8. Drizzle the tahini dressing over the salad and toss gently to coat all ingredients evenly.
9. Divide the salad among serving plates or bowls.
10. Top each serving with roasted cauliflower and chickpeas, and crispy tofu cubes.
11. Optional: sprinkle with toasted sesame seeds for added flavor and crunch.
12. Serve the Roasted Cauliflower and Chickpea Salad with Tofu immediately and enjoy this flavorful and nutritious dish!

Feel free to customize your Roasted Cauliflower and Chickpea Salad with Tofu by adding other ingredients such as roasted red bell pepper, avocado slices, or toasted nuts. You can also adjust the dressing to suit your taste preferences by adding more or less lemon juice, tahini, or maple syrup.

Greek Orzo Salad with Grilled Shrimp

Ingredients:

For the Grilled Shrimp:

- 1 lb large shrimp, peeled and deveined
- 2 tablespoons olive oil
- 2 cloves garlic, minced
- 1 teaspoon dried oregano
- Zest and juice of 1 lemon
- Salt and pepper to taste

For the Orzo Salad:

- 1 1/2 cups orzo pasta
- 2 cups cherry tomatoes, halved
- 1 English cucumber, diced
- 1/2 cup Kalamata olives, pitted and halved
- 1/2 cup crumbled feta cheese
- 1/4 cup chopped fresh parsley
- 1/4 cup chopped fresh dill
- Salt and pepper to taste

For the Greek Dressing:

- 1/4 cup extra virgin olive oil
- 2 tablespoons red wine vinegar
- 1 clove garlic, minced
- 1 teaspoon dried oregano
- Salt and pepper to taste

Instructions:

1. Preheat your grill or grill pan over medium-high heat.
2. In a large mixing bowl, combine the olive oil, minced garlic, dried oregano, lemon zest, lemon juice, salt, and pepper. Add the peeled and deveined shrimp to the bowl and toss to coat them evenly with the marinade. Let them marinate for about 15 minutes.

3. Thread the marinated shrimp onto skewers, if using, or place them directly on the grill. Grill the shrimp for about 2-3 minutes per side, or until they are pink and opaque. Once cooked, remove them from the grill and set aside.
4. Cook the orzo pasta according to package instructions until al dente. Drain and rinse under cold water to stop the cooking process. Let it cool slightly.
5. In a large salad bowl, combine the cooked orzo pasta, halved cherry tomatoes, diced cucumber, halved Kalamata olives, crumbled feta cheese, chopped fresh parsley, and chopped fresh dill. Season with salt and pepper to taste.
6. In a small bowl, whisk together the ingredients for the Greek dressing: extra virgin olive oil, red wine vinegar, minced garlic, dried oregano, salt, and pepper.
7. Drizzle the Greek dressing over the orzo salad and toss gently to coat all ingredients evenly.
8. Divide the orzo salad among serving plates or bowls.
9. Top each serving with grilled shrimp.
10. Serve the Greek Orzo Salad with Grilled Shrimp immediately and enjoy this flavorful and refreshing dish!

Feel free to customize your Greek Orzo Salad with Grilled Shrimp by adding other ingredients such as diced red onion, chopped bell peppers, or sliced avocado. You can also adjust the dressing to suit your taste preferences by adding more or less red wine vinegar, garlic, or herbs.

Asian-Inspired Tofu and Edamame Salad

Ingredients:

For the Tofu:

- 1 block (14 oz) firm tofu, drained and pressed
- 2 tablespoons soy sauce
- 1 tablespoon sesame oil
- 1 tablespoon rice vinegar
- 1 tablespoon honey or maple syrup
- 1 teaspoon grated ginger
- 1 clove garlic, minced
- Salt and pepper to taste

For the Salad:

- 4 cups mixed salad greens (such as lettuce, spinach, and arugula)
- 1 cup shelled edamame beans (thawed if frozen)
- 1 red bell pepper, thinly sliced
- 1 carrot, julienned or grated
- 1/4 cup sliced green onions
- 1/4 cup chopped fresh cilantro or parsley
- Optional: toasted sesame seeds for garnish

For the Dressing:

- 2 tablespoons soy sauce
- 2 tablespoons rice vinegar
- 1 tablespoon sesame oil
- 1 tablespoon honey or maple syrup
- 1 teaspoon grated ginger
- 1 clove garlic, minced
- 1 teaspoon sriracha or chili paste (optional, for heat)
- Salt and pepper to taste

Instructions:

1. Preheat your oven to 400°F (200°C).
2. Cut the pressed tofu into cubes and place them in a shallow dish.
3. In a small bowl, whisk together soy sauce, sesame oil, rice vinegar, honey or maple syrup, grated ginger, minced garlic, salt, and pepper. Pour the marinade over the tofu cubes, coating them evenly. Let them marinate for about 15-20 minutes.
4. Place the marinated tofu cubes on a baking sheet lined with parchment paper. Bake in the preheated oven for 20-25 minutes, or until the tofu is golden brown and slightly crispy on the outside.
5. In a large salad bowl, combine the mixed salad greens, shelled edamame beans, thinly sliced red bell pepper, julienned or grated carrot, sliced green onions, and chopped fresh cilantro or parsley.
6. In a small bowl, whisk together the ingredients for the dressing: soy sauce, rice vinegar, sesame oil, honey or maple syrup, grated ginger, minced garlic, sriracha or chili paste (if using), salt, and pepper.
7. Drizzle the dressing over the salad and toss gently to coat all ingredients evenly.
8. Divide the salad among serving plates or bowls.
9. Top each serving with baked tofu cubes.
10. Optional: sprinkle with toasted sesame seeds for added flavor and crunch.
11. Serve the Asian-Inspired Tofu and Edamame Salad immediately and enjoy this flavorful and nutritious dish!

Feel free to customize your Asian-Inspired Tofu and Edamame Salad by adding other ingredients such as sliced cucumber, shredded cabbage, or chopped peanuts. You can also adjust the dressing to suit your taste preferences by adding more or less soy sauce, honey, or sriracha.

Turkey and Apple Salad with Honey Mustard Dressing

Ingredients:

For the Salad:

- 2 cups cooked turkey breast, shredded or diced
- 2 medium apples, cored and thinly sliced
- 4 cups mixed salad greens (such as lettuce, spinach, and arugula)
- 1/2 cup sliced red onion
- 1/4 cup dried cranberries or raisins
- 1/4 cup chopped walnuts or pecans

For the Honey Mustard Dressing:

- 1/4 cup Dijon mustard
- 2 tablespoons honey
- 2 tablespoons apple cider vinegar
- 1/4 cup extra virgin olive oil
- Salt and pepper to taste

Instructions:

1. In a large salad bowl, combine the cooked turkey breast, thinly sliced apples, mixed salad greens, sliced red onion, dried cranberries or raisins, and chopped walnuts or pecans.
2. In a small bowl, whisk together the ingredients for the honey mustard dressing: Dijon mustard, honey, apple cider vinegar, extra virgin olive oil, salt, and pepper. Adjust the seasoning to taste.
3. Drizzle the honey mustard dressing over the salad and toss gently to coat all ingredients evenly.
4. Divide the salad among serving plates or bowls.
5. Serve the Turkey and Apple Salad with Honey Mustard Dressing immediately and enjoy this flavorful and nutritious dish!

Feel free to customize your Turkey and Apple Salad with Honey Mustard Dressing by adding other ingredients such as sliced cucumber, shredded carrots, or crumbled feta cheese. You can also adjust the dressing to suit your taste preferences by adding more or less honey, mustard, or vinegar.

Mediterranean Chickpea Salad with Feta

Ingredients:

For the Salad:

- 2 cans (15 oz each) chickpeas, drained and rinsed
- 1 cucumber, diced
- 1 pint cherry tomatoes, halved
- 1/2 red onion, thinly sliced
- 1/2 cup pitted Kalamata olives, halved
- 1/2 cup crumbled feta cheese
- 1/4 cup chopped fresh parsley
- 1/4 cup chopped fresh mint (optional)
- Salt and pepper to taste

For the Dressing:

- 1/4 cup extra virgin olive oil
- 2 tablespoons red wine vinegar
- 1 clove garlic, minced
- 1 teaspoon dried oregano
- Salt and pepper to taste

Instructions:

1. In a large salad bowl, combine the chickpeas, diced cucumber, halved cherry tomatoes, thinly sliced red onion, halved Kalamata olives, crumbled feta cheese, chopped fresh parsley, and chopped fresh mint (if using).
2. In a small bowl, whisk together the ingredients for the dressing: extra virgin olive oil, red wine vinegar, minced garlic, dried oregano, salt, and pepper.
3. Drizzle the dressing over the salad and toss gently to coat all ingredients evenly.
4. Season with additional salt and pepper to taste, if needed.
5. Serve the Mediterranean Chickpea Salad with Feta immediately, or refrigerate for at least 30 minutes to allow the flavors to meld before serving.
6. Enjoy this refreshing and flavorful salad as a light meal or as a side dish with grilled meats or seafood.

Feel free to customize your Mediterranean Chickpea Salad with Feta by adding other ingredients such as diced bell peppers, chopped cucumbers, or sliced radishes. You can also adjust the dressing to suit your taste preferences by adding more or less vinegar, garlic, or herbs.

Seared Tuna and Edamame Salad

Ingredients:

For the Seared Tuna:

- 2 tuna steaks, about 6 ounces each
- 2 tablespoons soy sauce
- 1 tablespoon sesame oil
- 1 tablespoon lime juice
- 1 teaspoon grated ginger
- 2 cloves garlic, minced
- Salt and pepper to taste
- 1 tablespoon sesame seeds (optional, for garnish)

For the Salad:

- 4 cups mixed salad greens (such as lettuce, spinach, and arugula)
- 1 cup shelled edamame beans (thawed if frozen)
- 1 carrot, julienned or grated
- 1 cucumber, thinly sliced
- 1/4 cup sliced radishes
- 1/4 cup sliced green onions
- 1 avocado, sliced
- 1 tablespoon chopped fresh cilantro or parsley (optional, for garnish)

For the Dressing:

- 2 tablespoons soy sauce
- 2 tablespoons rice vinegar
- 1 tablespoon sesame oil
- 1 tablespoon honey or maple syrup
- 1 teaspoon grated ginger
- 1 clove garlic, minced
- Salt and pepper to taste

Instructions:

1. In a shallow dish, whisk together soy sauce, sesame oil, lime juice, grated ginger, minced garlic, salt, and pepper. Place the tuna steaks in the marinade, turning to coat. Let them marinate for about 15-30 minutes.
2. In the meantime, prepare the salad ingredients. In a large salad bowl, combine the mixed salad greens, shelled edamame beans, julienned or grated carrot, thinly sliced cucumber, sliced radishes, sliced green onions, and sliced avocado.
3. In a small bowl, whisk together the ingredients for the dressing: soy sauce, rice vinegar, sesame oil, honey or maple syrup, grated ginger, minced garlic, salt, and pepper. Set aside.
4. Heat a skillet or grill pan over medium-high heat. Remove the tuna steaks from the marinade and discard any excess marinade. Sear the tuna steaks for about 2-3 minutes per side, or until they are seared on the outside but still pink in the center. Cooking time may vary depending on the thickness of the tuna steaks.
5. Remove the seared tuna steaks from the skillet and let them rest for a few minutes before slicing thinly.
6. Drizzle the dressing over the salad and toss gently to coat all ingredients evenly.
7. Divide the salad among serving plates or bowls. Top each serving with sliced seared tuna.
8. Optional: sprinkle with sesame seeds and chopped fresh cilantro or parsley for garnish.
9. Serve the Seared Tuna and Edamame Salad immediately and enjoy this flavorful and nutritious dish!

Feel free to customize your Seared Tuna and Edamame Salad by adding other ingredients such as bell peppers, cherry tomatoes, or sliced red onion. You can also adjust the dressing to suit your taste preferences by adding more or less soy sauce, honey, or ginger.

Southwest Quinoa Salad with Grilled Chicken

Ingredients:

For the Grilled Chicken:

- 2 boneless, skinless chicken breasts
- 2 tablespoons olive oil
- 1 tablespoon lime juice
- 1 teaspoon ground cumin
- 1 teaspoon chili powder
- 1/2 teaspoon garlic powder
- Salt and pepper to taste

For the Quinoa Salad:

- 1 cup quinoa, rinsed
- 2 cups water or chicken broth
- 1 can (15 oz) black beans, drained and rinsed
- 1 cup corn kernels (fresh, canned, or frozen)
- 1 red bell pepper, diced
- 1/4 cup diced red onion
- 1/4 cup chopped fresh cilantro
- 1 avocado, diced
- Juice of 1 lime
- Salt and pepper to taste

For the Dressing:

- 1/4 cup olive oil
- 2 tablespoons lime juice
- 1 teaspoon ground cumin
- 1/2 teaspoon chili powder
- 1/4 teaspoon garlic powder
- Salt and pepper to taste

Instructions:

1. Preheat your grill or grill pan over medium-high heat.
2. In a shallow dish, whisk together olive oil, lime juice, ground cumin, chili powder, garlic powder, salt, and pepper. Add the chicken breasts to the dish, turning to coat them evenly with the marinade. Let them marinate for about 15-30 minutes.
3. In the meantime, prepare the quinoa according to package instructions. Once cooked, fluff the quinoa with a fork and let it cool slightly.
4. Grill the marinated chicken breasts for about 6-8 minutes per side, or until they are cooked through and no longer pink in the center. Once cooked, remove them from the grill and let them rest for a few minutes before slicing thinly.
5. In a large mixing bowl, combine the cooked quinoa, black beans, corn kernels, diced red bell pepper, diced red onion, and chopped fresh cilantro.
6. In a small bowl, whisk together the ingredients for the dressing: olive oil, lime juice, ground cumin, chili powder, garlic powder, salt, and pepper.
7. Drizzle the dressing over the quinoa salad and toss gently to coat all ingredients evenly.
8. Add the diced avocado to the salad and squeeze the lime juice over it to prevent browning. Gently toss to combine.
9. Divide the quinoa salad among serving plates or bowls.
10. Top each serving with sliced grilled chicken.
11. Serve the Southwest Quinoa Salad with Grilled Chicken immediately and enjoy this delicious and nutritious dish!

Feel free to customize your Southwest Quinoa Salad with Grilled Chicken by adding other ingredients such as cherry tomatoes, diced jalapenos, or shredded cheese. You can also adjust the dressing to suit your taste preferences by adding more or less lime juice, cumin, or chili powder.

Spinach and Bacon Salad with Hard-Boiled Eggs

Ingredients:

For the Salad:

- 6 cups fresh spinach leaves, washed and dried
- 6 slices bacon, cooked until crispy and crumbled
- 4 hard-boiled eggs, peeled and sliced
- 1/2 cup sliced red onion
- 1/4 cup sliced almonds (optional)
- Salt and pepper to taste

For the Dressing:

- 3 tablespoons olive oil
- 2 tablespoons red wine vinegar
- 1 teaspoon Dijon mustard
- 1 teaspoon honey or maple syrup
- Salt and pepper to taste

Instructions:

1. In a large salad bowl, combine the fresh spinach leaves, crispy crumbled bacon, sliced hard-boiled eggs, sliced red onion, and sliced almonds (if using).
2. In a small bowl, whisk together the ingredients for the dressing: olive oil, red wine vinegar, Dijon mustard, honey or maple syrup, salt, and pepper.
3. Drizzle the dressing over the spinach and bacon salad and toss gently to coat all ingredients evenly.
4. Season with additional salt and pepper to taste, if needed.
5. Serve the Spinach and Bacon Salad with Hard-Boiled Eggs immediately as a side dish or as a light meal.

Enjoy this classic salad with its combination of fresh spinach, savory bacon, creamy hard-boiled eggs, and tangy dressing! Feel free to customize the salad by adding other ingredients such as sliced mushrooms, cherry tomatoes, or crumbled feta cheese.

www.ingramcontent.com/pod-product-compliance
Lightning Source LLC
LaVergne TN
LVHW061939070526
838199LV00060B/3878